Getting the Right Things Done

A leader's guide to planning and execution

by **Pascal Dennis**

Foreword by Jim Womack

Lean Enterprise Institute
Cambridge, MA, USA
lean.org

October 2009

Lean Enterprise Institute

Design by Off-Piste Design, Inc.
October 2009
ISBN: 0-9763152-6-2

Lean Enterprise Institute, Inc.
One Cambridge Center
Cambridge, MA 02142 USA
(t) 617-871-2900 • (f) 617-871-2999 • lean.org

Author Acknowledgments

I'm grateful to all the good people who helped me with this difficult project, and acknowledge them here: Jim Womack and Helen Zak, for believing in the "leader's guide" concept; Dave LaHote, for his insight into the heating, ventilation and air conditioning industry and the transformation process; Orest Fiume, for his insight into real-number accounting; George Taninecz, for quick, clean edits and big-picture perspective; Thomas and Jennifer Skehan, for marvelous graphics; Michael Brassard, friend, collaborator, and editor extraordinaire, for pushing so hard (merci, mon ami); all our reviewers for their time and care; and my dear wife, Pamela, who put up with my mock-complaints (*I'm a broken man ...*) and kept the proverbial home fires burning. I owe you a dinner (or 12) in Greektown.

In memory of Dr. Robert Guselle (1925–2005).
We miss you, Bob.

Publisher Acknowledgments

With gratitude to Gary Berndt, Jerry Bussell, Cynthia Massari Christie, Tom Ehrenfeld, Dan Jones, Dave LaHote, Dave Logozzo, Kathy Miller, Guy Parsons, Deb Porto, Russ Scaffede, John Shook, Thomas Skehan, George Taninecz, Jim Womack, and Helen Zak for providing their honest feedback and improvement suggestions throughout the development of this book. Thanks also to Paige Morency-Brassard for her artistic inspiration.

Foreword

Lean thinkers have many tools available today. Indeed, the Lean Enterprise Institute has provided a number of these. Value-stream maps. Guides to cell design. Instructions for pull systems. Advice on handling materials and information. Even guidance on looking at value streams and information and material flow between firms with shared value streams.

However, it is widely noted that the sum is less than the parts. With so many good tools available, we should have made much greater progress in creating lean enterprises. The problem is management. Specifically it's the tenacious hold of traditional mass production management with its top-down, manage-by-results mindset that never examines the process for deploying policy.

There have been policy management tools designed to counteract this bias, of course. Dozens of books on hoshin kanri (also called policy deployment) are available. And many of these contain valuable advice, in particular on selecting organizational objectives and getting alignment.

But again, the sum is less than the parts. Many organizations with elaborate policy deployment mechanisms in place never seem to actually deploy policy. They bog down selecting the right things to do and never get the right things done.

Years ago we observed that this does not seem to be a problem at Toyota. This firm is not only highly effective at selecting the right things to do— witness the brilliant decision to pursue hybrid technology when other companies were paralyzed—but is highly effective in getting the right things done once selected.

As we thought about creating a leader's guide for getting the right things done we naturally looked for someone familiar with the Toyota system. Indeed, we wanted someone who had not just studied it but actually used the Toyota method.

Fortunately, Pascal Dennis stepped forward. He was a manager at Toyota Motor Manufacturing Canada at a time of rapid expansion when many things needed to be done quickly and correctly. He learned firsthand how to apply Toyota's strategy deployment method in this continually changing environment. Since leaving Toyota he has learned how to teach the method by coaching senior managers in a wide range of industries from manufacturing to healthcare to construction.

In the pages ahead, Pascal will illustrate the method by telling the story of the imaginary (but very real) Atlas Industries as it switches from traditional planning methods to rigorous strategy deployment. He will explain in detail how you and your organization can get the right things done by applying the method consistently.

We are aware that few readers of this guide will be leading organizations exactly like Atlas. And many readers will be involved in operations far from traditional manufacturing, ranging from financial services to healthcare to maintenance. Other readers are likely to be concerned foremost with functional areas of their organizations: product development, purchasing, marketing, sales, finance, and so on. Toyota's planning and execution method applies to all industries and functions. It provides the same advantages in every application.

To help readers make the transition from Atlas to their reality, we have created a web page for this book at the LEI website (www.lean.org/grtd). It provides examples of strategy deployment in a range of environments. It also provides many of the forms described in this leader's guide along with answers by the author to reader questions.

While the method described in these pages is simple, applying it will be a considerable leap for most organizations. Given the nature and magnitude of your challenge, we are eager to hear about your successes as well as your difficulties and to connect you with others in the Lean Community tackling similar problems. Please contact us and the author by sending your comments and questions to grtd@lean.org. With a bit of practice and through wide sharing of experience, all of us can move steadily ahead in getting the right things done.

Jim Womack
Chairman, Lean Enterprise Institute
December 2006

Contents

Introduction

What is strategy deployment—and why should you care? Within Toyota it's known as *hoshin kanri*,[1] the planning and execution system that has guided the development of the world's most powerful production system. At Toyota Motor Manufacturing Canada plant in Cambridge, Ontario, strategy deployment steered us through the chaos and stress of continual expansion. In 10 years we grew from a cornfield to a 3,000-person company making 230,000 cars per year.

Remarkably, in Cambridge our safety, quality, cost, and throughput results kept improving, and we were showered with awards. The system kept us humble. "How can they give *us* an award?" we'd wonder. "We have so many problems." It was quite a journey. Only now, years later, am I able to grasp what really happened, how we avoided catastrophe, and got so strong. It was my blind luck to work with a master trainer. (If you see this, Shin-san, I am in your debt.)

The past six years, I have been the *sensei*,[2] teaching the system *outside* Toyota, to both automotive and nonautomotive manufacturers, and to the process, service, and construction industries. Each implementation has deepened my understanding. What have I learned? Each company and sector is different, and most companies are *not* Toyota. We must tailor the planning and execution system to fit the business *as it is*, warts and all.

But why should you care? Well, strategy deployment will focus and align your activities, and allow you to respond quickly to threats and opportunities. Moreover, it's a *human* system. People respond because it acknowledges their individuality. With strategy deployment, we don't *tell*—we *ask* questions. We don't *command*—we *engage*. Our people are not human *resources*—they're *human* resources. Most important, we try not to bore with meaningless data—we try to tell interesting *stories*.

1. Also known as hoshin management, policy management, and policy deployment.
2. *Sensei* means teacher, mentor, or one who has gone before.

Strategy deployment is the antithesis to "command and control," still our predominant mental model and the reason the cartoon *Dilbert* is so popular. Command and control can suck the zest and meaning out of work. Insidious, it lives in the minds of supervisors, managers, and executives. Once we're promoted, we think our job is telling people what to do. "Very strange," my *sensei* once said. "In North America you manage business the way the Soviets managed their economy."

If you're a manufacturer facing low-cost global producers or other company-killing threats, strategy deployment can save the jobs that sustain your community. These days, manufacturers have little room for error. The ship is in the deep water and the storm shows no sign of abating.

But maybe you're not a manufacturer. Maybe you're a service provider, a software developer, a bank, a hospital, an insurance company. The storms are no less threatening. You might be facing your own challenges. Jobs that seemed secure just a few years ago are melting away—customer service, software development, engineering, research and development, and accounting jobs.

Strategy deployment is especially important for lean practitioners because it ensures that "lean" is aimed at the heart of the enterprise. Lean thinking begins by defining value—what's important to the customer. If lean serves the core needs of the customer—safety, quality, delivery, and cost—and is introduced at the highest levels of the organization, it's forever. By contrast, if lean is peripheral or introduced at lower organizational levels, it'll have a limited half-life—a major loss, given the exceptional track record of lean thinking.

Strategy deployment can also keep lean practitioners focused on the prize —creating value for the customer. Sometimes we forget that the elegant lean tools—value-stream mapping, standardized work, pull systems, and so on—are means to this end, and not ends in themselves.

Our improvement paradigm remains:

- ⊙ Stabilize,
- ⊙ Flow,
- ⊙ Pull, and
- ⊙ Improve the system (seek perfection).

Our engine is strategy deployment, through which we align, focus, and engage our team members. But unlike conventional planning systems, our emphasis is *deployment*—not selection—and deployment is difficult.

This book is intended for leaders at all levels and across all industries—from CEOs to frontline team leaders—and will help answer the following questions about deployment:

- ⊙ What are the nuts and bolts of strategy deployment?
- ⊙ What does an implementation look and feel like?
- ⊙ What are the underlying mental models and how are they different?
- ⊙ What kind of management is required?

I've tried to describe how strategy deployment might be implemented in a manufacturing plant. It could just as easily have been a hospital, laboratory, or an insurance company. Experience has taught me that there is no one best way. It all depends on the need. Think of it as customized standardized work.

Japanese is a metaphorical language. Hoshin kanri has several meanings, including "shiny metal" and "compass." My favorite is "ship in a storm going in the right direction." We're all in the deep water now, and the storm is raging. The waters may get even rougher. But there is a better way to navigate. Having a sensei certainly helps, but you may not have one. This guide and its protagonist, John Karras, can fill that role.

The young investment banker sat down opposite Bill Harman.

"Do you want to see the factory?" Harman asked.

"Not particularly."

"How will you know what the company's worth?"

"It's all just paper, Mr. Harman."

Harman looked through the reinforced glass wall of his office to the factory floor below. They were starting back up after the lunch break.

"So you're offering me $250 million."

"That's right, Mr. Harman."

"What's going to happen to my company?"

"We'll keep the distribution network, and do the manufacturing overseas. We might keep some design work in North America."

"Labor arbitrage," said Harman.

"That's right," said the banker.

"But labor is a small part of the total cost. What about the time on the water? What about the benefit of having a local supplier who knows your business and who'll work with you?"

"Mr. Harman, if that's true," said the banker, "then why aren't you making any money?"

Chapter 1
Getting Started

It was early Monday morning. John Karras, president and chief operating officer of Atlas Industries, was watching a changeover at the new Shultz stacking machine when his cell phone began buzzing. It was Bill Harman, Atlas' owner and CEO. Bill was semiretired; his main interests were philanthropy, racehorses, and his seven grandchildren. Karras ran the business; Harman checked in weekly. But Harman was always looking for opportunities. He had the business in his blood. "Karras! Guess who I played golf with this weekend?"

"Tiger Woods?"

"Nah, Jack Henderson. And guess what? They want us back—preferred supplier, air quality systems! What do you think of that?"

Henderson Controls was one of the country's biggest manufacturers of heating, ventilation, and air conditioning (HVAC) systems. They supplied the residential, commercial, and industrial sectors. When Henderson Controls dropped Atlas five years ago—for a low-cost overseas producer— it had triggered the crisis that eventually brought Karras to the company.

"That's great, Bill," said Karras. "Does Jack understand we're not in the commodity business anymore?"

"Yes, he does," said Harman. "He says he's impressed with what we've achieved. He wants to collaborate on UV air treatment systems and whole-house humidifiers. That means a long-term partnership and decent margins."

"Hallelujah!" Karras exclaimed.

"Absolutely," Harman added. "Indoor air quality has been a big problem for them—the mold-spore issue, kids' allergies, and so on. It's cost them a bundle—rework, lost business, and a few lawsuits, too. Low-cost suppliers can make basic coils and condensers, but can they work with you to provide healthier air? Can they help improve the entire system? Doesn't sound like it."

"Labor cost isn't everything," said Karras. "Henderson is learning that. This is a great opportunity, Bill. *Speed—Cost—Innovation*!"

"You were prescient, John, a regular Greek oracle."

Harman was proud of all that Atlas had achieved over the past five years. They enjoyed double-digit growth in revenue and EBIT[1]. They were no longer a supplier of commodities like evaporator coils and condensers. Now they worked with customers to improve the entire HVAC system, giving people the gift of healthy and comfortable air.

Losing the Henderson account years ago had triggered a personal crisis for Harman. He'd almost sold the company. "Who am I? What do I believe in?" he had asked himself. In Karras he recognized a kindred spirit, someone who had asked those same questions, and an exceptionally capable leader. Harman still remembered how he offered Karras the job of president and COO. Had it really been five years?

. . . .

"A Chicago holding company has offered to buy Atlas Industries," Harman said. "*$250 million*. My children want me to sell. But my grandfather started this company, and it's been my whole life. I'm already rich. What am I going to do—play golf all day? And if I sell, what'll happen to our people? I'll tell you. Half of them will lose their jobs because the holding company is going to move production offshore.

1. Earnings before interest and taxes.

"Maybe someday I *will* sell," Harman continued. "But it'll be to a local owner or maybe to an ESOP[2]—someone who will keep the jobs in the community. One last thing: I don't want this place to lose money. I want this place to *make* money—for me, for my grandkids, for everyone involved. I'm tired of playing defense. Let's turn this around."

Harman looked at Karras closely. "Are you in?"

"Why not," answered Karras.

And that's where our story begins.

Welcome to Atlas Industries—Five Years Ago

Atlas Industries manufactured evaporator coils, condensers, and heat exchangers for the residential and light industrial HVAC[3] markets. The company sold custom coils directly to OEM[4] HVAC manufacturers, and standard coils to wholesalers, which in turn sold to dealers and installers. There was a single, 500,000-square-foot manufacturing plant collocated with head office, several warehouses, and distribution centers. Annual revenue was about $250 million; EBIT was less than 2%. Atlas employed about 800 team members; about 650 were hourly, the rest were salaried. Atlas was the biggest employer in the county and had a long history of community service.

Atlas was caught between a proverbial rock and a hard place—price competition from global producers and cost spikes in aluminum, copper, steel, and other raw materials. Atlas' core products were becoming commodities. Overseas competitors were proving adept at manufacturing the six or eight core designs that comprised the bulk of the residential business. OEMs demanded annual cost-downs and used aggressive tactics like internet auctions to intensify the pressure on suppliers. Wholesalers were less price-conscious and open to custom design, but demanded quality and quick response.

2. Employee stock ownership plan.
3. Heating, ventilation, and air conditioning.
4. Original equipment manufacturer.

The HVAC market was hungry for innovation. Mold spores and other bioallergens were degrading indoor air quality and, in some cases, property values and human health. Efficiency was another important market driver. Innovative coil geometries could both improve heat-transfer efficiency and reduce the condensation that encouraged mold growth. But Atlas Industries had difficulty launching interesting and profitable new products; the sales force had little to get excited about.

In the Atlas factory, there were nagging machine availability issues. Stacking, brazing, and endforming machines; braze ovens; and leak testers broke down frequently. Changing over from one product to another could take hours. The manufacturing team ran large batches, *just in case*. Scrap was another sore spot. Wrong and missing parts and labels, system damage, leaks, and other defects kept recurring. They also kept running out of parts, though there were parts all over the place. Morale, once a strong point, was deteriorating; absenteeism and employee turnover were increasing.

The tools of lean production—aka the Toyota Production System—had been implemented in the factory with some success. Current- and future-state value-stream maps[5] had been developed for the residential evaporator-coil value stream—and everyone agreed that mapping was a useful exercise. Visual management and a 5S system[6] had been implemented, which had improved safety and housekeeping.

Kaizen events—also known as rapid improvement events—were held every few months. Some previously isolated processes were now grouped in U-shaped cells with some semblance of continuous flow.[7]

---

5. A diagram or map for identifying every step involved in the material and information flows needed to bring a product from order to delivery. For a detailed description of value-stream mapping, see: Mike Rother and John Shook, *Learning to See* (Cambridge, MA, Lean Enterprise Institute, 1999).
6. 5S is a system of workplace organization and standardization. The five components of 5S are sort, set in order, shine, standardize, and sustain.
7. Producing or moving one item at a time (or a small batch of items) through a series of processing steps as continuously as possible. See: Mike Rother and Rick Harris, *Creating Continuous Flow* (Cambridge, MA, Lean Enterprise Institute, 2001).

Standardized work had been developed in the final assembly department, and team members were trained. Rudimentary pull systems[8] between the factory supermarket and production cells also had been piloted with modest success. People had begun to experience the power of flow, pull, and standardization.

But the lean tools had been hard to *sustain*: Instability crept in. Machines broke down. There were part shortages. Team members did workarounds. Inventory mushroomed. Atlas was meeting customer delivery targets—but only by running continuous Saturday overtime and expediting shipments. "We're getting things done," thought Harman. "But are we getting the *right* things done?"

In summary, lean tools and serial kaizen events had resulted in spot improvements but no sustained breakthrough. The most important value streams hadn't really changed. Something was missing: a way of focusing and aligning the efforts of good people, and a delivery system, something that would direct the tools to the right places.

Atlas had a new president and COO in Karras, formerly general manager of a Toyota supplier. Function heads, called "directors" at Atlas, were accustomed to Harman's hands-off approach. For a month or so, it was business as usual. Karras sat in on management meetings in each functional area, and spent a lot of time on the shop floor. Then he called a management team meeting, saying, "Please show me this year's strategies and your current condition."

Almost all the directors were smart, hard-working, and ambitious. But they were neither aligned nor focused; they were good people working in silos. The Atlas strategic planning process was, in effect, a budget development process. Directors understood this and jockeyed for funds whether or not they needed them. Atlas Industries' annual strategy was,

8. A method of production control in which downstream activities signal their needs to upstream activities. For detailed descriptions of pull systems, see: Art Smalley, *Creating Level Pull* (Cambridge, MA, Lean Enterprise Institute, 2004), and Rick Harris et al, *Making Materials Flow* (Cambridge, MA, Lean Enterprise Institute, 2003).

in effect, whatever they spent money on. The management team was acutely aware of the company's problems. Nobody, except for Harman and Karras, knew about the holding company's offer to buy.

Atlas Industries

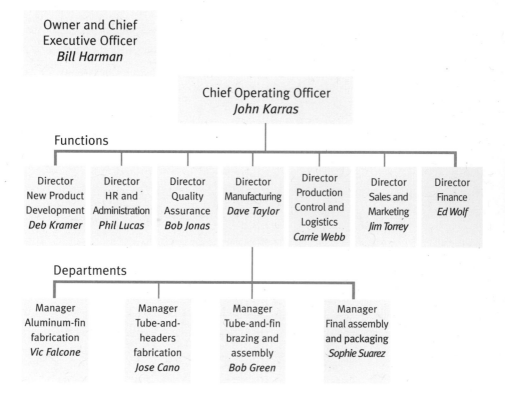

So there they all sat in the boardroom: oak paneling, fruit, pastries, and coffee. Karras sat up front with Harman and watched as Deb Kramer, director of New Product Development (NPD) got up and made her presentation: PowerPoint® slides and plenty of them. She went on about their new process and how it would improve lead time and manufacturability.

Then Phil Lucas, director of HR and Administration, got up and fired up his PowerPoint® presentation. More chart junk and PowerPoint® fluff. He talked about new OSHA regulations and the new international health and safety system standard. Bob Jonas, director of Quality Assurance (QA), got up next and showed a bunch of slides about international quality system standards and QA's auditing strategy.

And that's when Karras got up, walked over to the projector, and turned it off. "Let's just talk about our business," he said.

PowerPoint® Fluff

Less Is More

This simple aphorism, attributed to Robert Browning, applies in manufacturing, sports, and the arts. The fewer moving parts, the better the engine—or golf swing. Clear, simple sentences are the best ones.

Complexity reflects a primitive state; simplicity marks the end of a process of refining.

Winston Churchill said that to deliver a two-hour speech he needed 10 minutes of preparation, but to speak for 10 minutes he needed two hours of preparation.

Silence—*What's this guy up to?* The directors looked over at Harman—nothing. Karras spoke plainly. "Low-cost global producers are eating our lunch—and the bag it came in. We've just lost Henderson Controls, our biggest account. We've become a commodity supplier, which means more losses are in the pipeline. And yet, we have no *focus*, and we are not *aligned*."

The directors looked at one another. This guy didn't waste any time.

"We're also plagued by *unstable processes*. We make a lot of junk; our machines keep breaking down. We meet our delivery schedules only by running continuous overtime and expediting shipments. Our factory and supply chain are swimming in inventory—yet we keep running out of parts. Process instability may be an even *bigger* problem outside of manufacturing. Why does it take so long to get a new product to market? How capable is our training and development process? Why the turnover, especially in critical positions?

"None of the dots are connected," Karras continued. "NPD, HR, and QA are inextricably linked, yet there's no mention of shared goals and activities. I don't mean to pick on anyone. I'm sure the problems span all functions. Another thing: No more PowerPoint® fluff. Your strategies should be clear, simple stories on one page. If you can't tell your story on one page, you probably don't understand it. Less is more."

Karras continued: "We're going to learn and apply a powerful planning and execution system. It's called 'hoshin kanri.' I know that's a mysterious term, so I just call it 'strategy deployment.' It saved my last company. We're going to focus and align our activities around our business need. We're going to extend lean thinking across the enterprise."

The body language around the room was mixed. Some directors seemed relaxed. Maybe this guy would turn out all right. Others sat poker-faced, with their arms crossed.

Harman had the final word. "As you may have gathered, Mr. Karras is a straight shooter. We've been kidding ourselves for too long. I'm sick of it, and I'm sick of losing. Let's get going."

In the ensuing months, Karras taught the management team the components of strategy deployment:

- Agreement on the organization's strategic and philosophical "*True North.*"

- *Plan-Do-Check-Adjust*—the scientific method.

- The *management process* comprising the micro, annual, and macro Plan-Do-Check-Adjust cycles.

- *Catchball*—the process of gaining alignment by having frank conversations about what's important with your colleagues and team members.

- *Deployment leader concept*—the metaphor that dissolves silos and opens the door to cross-functionality.

- *A3 thinking*—the storytelling approach to planning and execution.

Karras had fun with language: "The veracity of an answer is inversely proportional to its length!" Candor and good humor were the essence of his style, together with an underlying consideration for people. He began to earn their trust.

Atlas Industries Manufacturing Processes and Structure

Atlas Industries manufacturing processes comprise:[9]

⊙ *Aluminum-fin fabrication*: Thin aluminum strips (fins) are cut, punched, and roll-formed. Fins maximize the surface area available for heating and cooling. Fin-fabrication machines, like stackers, are large, prone to breakdowns, and entail long changeovers. Common quality problems include leaks and damage to fins.

⊙ *Tube-and-header fabrication*: Headers made of aluminum, copper, and occasionally steel are cut, formed, and brazed. Headers direct refrigerant in and out of coils and condensers through tubes and hoses. Tubing, usually copper or aluminum, is cut, bent, and brazed. Brazing can be manual or automatic (e.g., rotary tables or oven brazing of headers).

⊙ *Tube-and-fin brazing and assembly*: Components are assembled into a finished coil using some type of structural frame (called an "A" frame in residential applications, due to its shape). Atlas uses both brazing and welding for this purpose. Leak testing, a critical quality control step, is often a bottleneck. Both air/water and "sniffer" leak testers are temperamental and prone to breakdown.

⊙ *Final assembly and packaging*: Finished coils are fitted with fasteners, drain plugs, and other hardware. Final assembly also entails labeling and packaging,

9. If you're not a manufacturer, don't be concerned with understanding the processes; focus on the strategy deployment principles, which apply across businesses and industries.

both critical to quality. The wrong label can mean a suction hose on the left side—when you need it on the right side. Packaging protects aluminum fins from damage and prevents this common quality problem. Other quality problems in final assembly include leaks and wrong or missing parts and labels.

Atlas Industries—Manufacturing

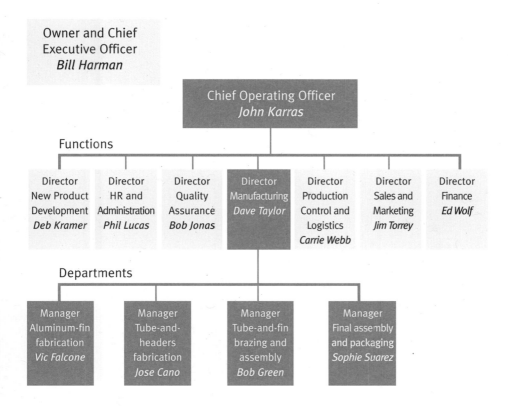

Owner and Chief Executive Officer
Bill Harman

Chief Operating Officer
John Karras

Functions

| Director New Product Development *Deb Kramer* | Director HR and Administration *Phil Lucas* | Director Quality Assurance *Bob Jonas* | Director Manufacturing *Dave Taylor* | Director Production Control and Logistics *Carrie Webb* | Director Sales and Marketing *Jim Torrey* | Director Finance *Ed Wolf* |

Departments

| Manager Aluminum-fin fabrication *Vic Falcone* | Manager Tube-and-headers fabrication *Jose Cano* | Manager Tube-and-fin brazing and assembly *Bob Green* | Manager Final assembly and packaging *Sophie Suarez* |

The Big Questions

Describe your company's planning and execution system.

What are its strong points?

What are its weak points?

How would you improve the system?

Describe your company's improvement activities (lean or otherwise) over the past five years.

What worked, and why did it work?

What didn't work, and why not?

What would you do differently?

"What business are we in, Bill?" Karras asked, turning out of the parking lot. They were driving to a customer site—part of what Karras called "my presidential diagnosis."

"Why, we're in the business of making money," Harman replied.

"Really?" said Karras. "I thought our business was making HVAC products that delight our customers."

"Isn't it the same thing?" Harman replied.

"What would our team members say?"

Harman looked out the window. "I get it. It isn't the same thing at all."

"How leaders *think* matters," said Karras. "Everything else follows."

They drove in silence a while.

"John, I've been thinking like this all my life. How does an old dog change?"

"We need to talk about our mental models," Karras said.

"Do you find it difficult, John?"

"You bet," Karras replied.

"Well, maybe there's hope for me."

Chapter 2
Mental Models

They started in November. Karras asked Ed Wolf, the director of Finance, to drive the implementation of strategy deployment across Atlas Industries. Karras had found that accountants often had a good understanding of the Plan-Do-Check-Adjust cycle, around which Atlas would structure its planning and execution system. Karras asked Dave Taylor and Sophie Suarez, Dave's most experienced manager, to drive implementation in Manufacturing.

"We need to grasp our current condition," said Karras, "so we're going to the 'gemba.' That just means 'real place'—where the action happens. For us that means going to the factory floor, the New Product Development lab, customer sites, and so on."

Their first meeting was held on the factory floor. They "walked the process" from receipt of raw materials to shipping of finished goods. Karras stopped frequently to talk with team members and to pick up garbage off the floor. Sophie, Ed, and Dave, embarrassed, did the same.

Dave asked Karras whether they should do more training in the tools of lean production. Team members had found value-stream mapping and 5S training helpful. They were in aluminum-fin fabrication, watching a stacking machine changeover.

"Tools are important," Karras said. "But the tools make a *management system*, and a *way of thinking* underlies the tools." He drew it out for them in his notebook. "Lean transformations most often fail because people have the wrong mental models."

Strategy Deployment and the Finance Team

When implementing strategy deployment, engage the Finance team early on. Too often this group is relegated to the lowly position of "bean counters," rather than its proper role: trusted adviser and business partner. In my experience, once members of the Finance team grasp the benefits of lean thinking, they are among its strongest advocates.

Moreover, there are important similarities between strategy deployment and financial planning. Both entail an annual planning cycle and a periodic checking process during which targets and actual results are compared and for which variances are accounted. Accountants also understand the importance of the story behind the numbers.

Finally, strategy deployment needs Finance to cut through the fog of standard cost accounting and translate lean gains into real numbers (a topic Atlas Industries will have to address). For example, if through lean activities we stabilize our processes and equipment, we'll be able to reduce inventory and order-to-cash cycle time. We also will free up cash and capacity, which will allow us to chase new business. But reducing inventory will negatively affect the income statement at first. We may be stronger, quicker, and more productive, but the scoreboard tells us we're doing worse! Such are the vagaries of standard cost accounting, which the profession is addressing.[1]

1. For more information on these and other accounting issues, see: Orest Fiume and Jean E. Cunningham with Emily Adams, *Real Numbers: Management Accounting in a Lean Organization* (Managing Times Press, 2003), and Brian Maskell and Bruce Baggaley, *Practical Lean Accounting: A Proven System for Measuring and Managing in a Lean Enterprise* (University Park, IL, Productivity Press, 2003).

Thinking Foundation

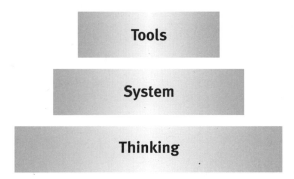

"What do you mean by *mental models*?" Sophie asked.

"It's a person's assumptions about how the world works, based on their experience, upbringing, and temperament," Karras said. "Mental models are the glasses we all wear, which filter and often distort reality. For example, at a dentists' convention, people look at one another's teeth; at a hair stylist convention, they look at hair—different perceptions of the same reality. You and I go into a crowded party, pick up the same sensory data—but pick out different faces. The world we see is our own."

They mulled it over as they walked over to the tube-and-header fabrication department. Karras went over to the scrap bins to examine the day's casualties. "These shouldn't be hidden away," he said. "We need a table here displaying today's scrap and a daily review process. Problems are treasures." Dave made a note.

"So mental models are important," Karras went on, "because they affect what we *see* and what we *do*. We have to talk about them, so we can understand and improve them. Until we accept the fact that the constraint is between our ears, nothing will change.

Problems Are Treasures

"Mental models can be simple generalizations," Karras added, "like 'Fred is a funny guy' or complex theories of management. Key point: the right mental models are as set in stone for management as physical laws are for engineers—because they're based on universal principles."

"That's a mouthful," said Ed.

"Yes, it is," Karras grinned. "For example, if you're designing a machine, force equals mass times acceleration. It's not negotiable. If you fail to respect the $F = ma$ law, the machine won't work and might blow up. Similarly, if you're a manager, you *go and see* with your own eyes—like we're doing now. It's also not negotiable—if you want to be a successful.

"Here's a concrete example. As I said, problems are treasures; we have to make them visible. But can anyone tell how the tube-and-header fab department is doing today? Are we ahead or behind? What kinds of problems are we having? There's no indication. Does that mean everything is OK?"

"Visual management needs to be improved," Dave said sheepishly.

They walked over to the tube-and-fin braze and assembly department to look at the rotary torch brazing machines. Karras asked Ed to record cycle times while he continued their lesson.

"Leadership is about *language*. Semantics, the study of the relationship between language and meaning, is a critical skill. Out of the chaotic jumble of words, data, and perceptions, leaders must find the two or three messages that have *meaning*. Thus, the leader defines reality."

"But, with respect, it's all just *words*, John," Dave said. "Tomorrow we have to make condensers, heat exchangers, and evaporator coils. How do words help us?"

"Good question, Dave," Karras replied. "Who can answer it?"

"Well, I guess, words reflect mental models," Sophie offered, "which determine behavior."

Karras nodded. "Here's another example: every day production team members face a whirlwind—changing manpower, machinery, methods, and materials. They look to their team leaders. If their team leaders believe that problems are *garbage*, their language will reflect it. So we'll never talk about our problems, let alone solve them. And where do team leaders get their direction? From you and me.

"As Dave suggested, the leader has to be at home at the level of *experience* as well as the level of *thought*. Action without theory is aimless; theory without action is lifeless. Effective leaders move fluidly up and down a ladder of abstraction, between lower-level facts and higher-level concepts. If you speak at high levels of abstraction without having reasoned your way to them from lower levels, what you say is unlikely to be founded in fact. Similarly, if you're mired in lower-level data unable to extract the meaning, what you say is unlikely to motivate team members."

They walked over to final assembly and packaging, Sophie's department. Ed and Sophie were intrigued with these ideas; Dave was struggling. "There are 10 or 12 core mental models that we need to get down cold," Karras went on. "Even small misalignments can greatly affect behavior. That's why a great sensei continually reinforces the basics."

"What are the critical mental models, John?" Dave asked.

"You already know some of them," Karras replied. "In your value-stream mapping workshops, you learned about the value stream and about flow and pull. Who can explain these mental models?"

"The value stream is a series of steps to bring a product or service to the customer," said Sophie. "You start by defining value from the customer's point of view."

"Flow means make one, move one," said Dave, "as opposed to making big batches that sit in long queues; the smaller the batch, the shorter the lead time."

"And pull means don't make one until the downstream customer wants it," said Ed, who was completing his time study. "The magic of pull is that it controls work-in-process. Inventory costs, operating expenses, and lead times drop. When it works right, it's magic."

Karras nodded, impressed. "Now let's talk about planning and execution. What mental models support strategy deployment? And how do they differ from those of conventional planning?"

They found an old flip chart by a packaging machine and went to work. Karras began by contrasting two core mental models, which he called *Thou Shalt* and *What Do You Think?*

"*Thou Shalt* means the leader is the boss," Karras said, "and it's a debilitating mental model. When you tell people what to do, their minds close. You lose their experience, knowledge, and creativity. The more you tell them what to do, the more their minds close. End result? *Dilbert.*

"By contrast, *What Do You Think?* means the leader is the teacher. Like an open door, asking questions invites people in. It's called the Socratic method of teaching. The underlying message is 'I value your opinion.' A benevolent cycle results: people feel good so they get involved, which makes them feel even better. The result is that companies like Toyota get millions of improvement suggestions from team members."

Karras then described two different strategy-deployment approaches— conventional vs. lean. It wasn't as difficult as they thought. Even Dave got into it. When they were done, Ed gathered up the chart paper and got it transcribed. In the months to come, they'd refer to these notes repeatedly.

"That's enough for today," said Karras. "There are more mental models, which I'll point out as we come to them. Tomorrow we meet in the New Product Development lab at 10:00 a.m. I've asked Deb Kramer to give us an overview of the NPD process. There's also an NPD report-out followed by a team meeting. The day after tomorrow, we're visiting customers with Jim Torrey."

Karras had unsettled Dave, who had always been a man of action and uncomfortable with words. His nickname was "Get'er Done Dave." Karras had said, "Action without theory is aimless." That's me, thought Dave. He felt responsible for Atlas' problems—but didn't know what to do. Would Karras help me, he wondered, or would he think me incompetent?

Conventional-Planning Mental Models

1
Thou shalt! Leader = dictator.

2
Only grunts go to the floor.

3
We have some standards—not sure where they are or if they're followed.

4
Move the metal. Make the numbers.

Good luck!

boxes

5
Don't get caught holding the bag.

6
Specialists solve problems using complex methods.

Going nowhere fast.

Lean Mental Models

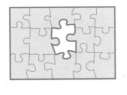

1

What do you think?
Leader = teacher.

2

Go see for yourself.

3

We have simple, visual standards
for all important things.

4

Stop production so that production
doesn't have to stop. *Don't ship junk.*

5

Make problems visible.

6

Everyone solves problems using
simple methods.

Getting the right things done.

The View from Above

Harman and Karras were having drinks at the Imperial Bar & Grill, a legendary local joint.

"John, now that you know the players," said Harman, "what do you think?"

"I think they're good people who want to do the right thing," Karras said. "I can work with them."

"What's the next five years look like?"

Karras took a pull on his beer. "If it goes like I hope, it's a four-step recipe, Bill. We need to *stabilize, flow, pull,* and *seek perfection.* It'll take three to five years. This year we'll focus on *stability*—which means stabilizing the four Ms of manpower, methods, machinery, and materials."

"Makes sense," Harman replied. "Without stability, nothing else will take root. I'm starting to understand *flow* and *pull.* But what do you mean by the last part?"

"Seek perfection—it means get better each day, and never give up."

Harman nodded. "So what's next?"

"We're going to define our objectives, then develop and deploy strategies to achieve them. Companies spend most of their time selecting the perfect objective—and precious little time on deployment. We won't make that mistake. Anybody can make a plan; but deployment is the hard part."

Selection vs. Deployment

Conventional planning systems emphasize selection, but have little to say about deployment. We spend most of our planning time answering questions like: What threats and opportunities exist in our environment? What are the strengths and weaknesses of our organization? What are our values and social responsibilities? Based on our answers, we evaluate and select strategies.

Now what?

Strategy deployment asks the same good questions, but emphasizes deployment. "Any damn fool can make a plan. It's the execution that gets you screwed up."[3]

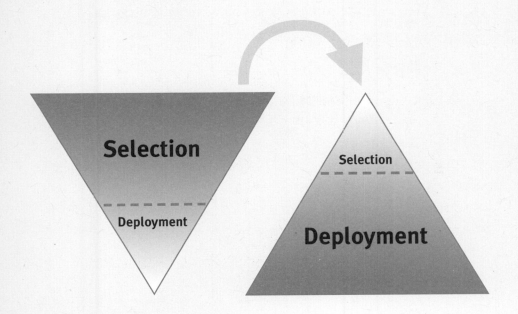

3. Henry Mintzberg, quoting a U.S. Army officer in *The Rise and Fall of Strategic Planning*, (New York, The Free Press, 1994).

The Big Questions

Describe three existing mental models at your organization.

Describe your company's mental models regarding
planning and execution.

What mental models help you achieve your goals?
How do they help you?

Which mental models hinder your ability to achieve goals?
How do they hinder you?

"5S is the foundation of the Toyota Production System," a manager had said. 5S training improved things for a while, then they regressed. So they tried *standardized* work. But that didn't seem to stick either.

"Standardized work depends on stable equipment," declared the maintenance manager. So they tried to implement *Total Productive Maintenance*. Things got better for a while, then slid back.

"Well, you're all wrong," another manager told them. "Lean production won't work unless there's *employee involvement*. So they put in a suggestion program and ran a series of kaizen events with few lasting benefits.

"What did you expect?" said the Quality Assurance manager. "You've got to have *error-proofing*. It's a pillar of the system."

And that's when the director pulled the plug on lean training. Afterward they said, "We tried lean production, but it didn't really work."

Chapter 3
Management Systems

Sophie Suarez, Ed Wolf, and Dave Taylor met Karras in New Product Development. This was the first in a series of meetings in which they would be trying to grasp the inner workings of Atlas Industries' major processes.

Deb Kramer, the director, gave them an overview of Atlas Industries' NPD process, and then they attended the NPD status report. Deb was new and was working hard to make her mark. NPD had never been an important function at Atlas. Afterward Karras thanked the NPD team for their presentation and asked a number of questions, including:

⊙ What is NPD's capacity for new projects?

⊙ What was throughput the past 12 months?

⊙ How many new projects are currently in the pipeline?

⊙ What are typical lead times for new products?

⊙ What is the current utilization rate of NPD engineers?

⊙ How many projects per engineer?

⊙ Where was the waste in the NPD process?

⊙ What were they doing about it?

The NPD team struggled with these questions; Deb promised Karras clear answers by the end of the week.

Following the NPD meeting, Karras, Ed, John, Sophie, and Deb had a post mortem. "Deb, it's not my intent to pick on NPD. Every leader in our company, from team leaders to directors, needs to know his or her capacity, throughput, and cycle time. They also need to know what's working and not working—at all times. I call it *zone control*," Karras said.

"John, I agree with what you're saying," said Deb. "Here's our biggest problem. We have *far too many* new projects in our pipeline—we're far above our capacity. But people keep throwing things into the NPD hopper. Dave, with respect, you do it all the time. And Mr. Harman is even worse. So each engineer works on eight or nine projects at once. And they're not even *cool* projects—they're *boring*. My people are burning out; some of them have already bailed. We've got other problems, too."

Zone Control

Visual Management in NPD

"We need to make NPD's problems visible," said Karras. "For example, I can imagine a race track or a football field on one wall showing what phase each project is at with, say, magnetic comment boxes summing up the main problems and countermeasures. That might also be a good way of controlling the number of projects. You can't add a new project until a space has opened up on the wall. In the interim, I'll talk to Harman and the directors about NPD's capacity issues."

Deb took copious notes. NPD at Atlas had always been limited to design tweaks that marginally improved energy efficiency. Deb told Karras about some of the opportunities she saw in the HVAC industry. Karras was impressed and said, "Deb, I'd like the NPD team to play a much bigger role. It'll be a challenge, but fun, too.

"One last thing," Karras added. "What's with all these cubicles? NPD folks need to be elbow-to-elbow. Also, where are the Sales and Marketing and Manufacturing folks? They should be here for NPD report-outs."

Deb smiled, "I've been saying that since I got here."

Karras, Ed, Dave, and Sophie then walked over to see the leak-testing machines, which had been acting up again. "Yesterday we talked about lean mental models," Karras said. "Any questions?"

"I think I understand lean mental models a little better," Ed said. "But you also said that lean tools make a *management system*. What do you mean by that?"

What Is a Management System?

Karras usually responded to questions with *more* questions. After a lengthy question-and-answer series, Dave, Ed, and Sophie understood that a management system was a *series of integrated parts with a clearly defined goal*.

To illustrate, Karras drew the "solar system model" on a flip chart. "If we're going to think and plan around here, we'll need some new whiteboards and flip charts. Now imagine you're the equipment maintenance manager at a hospital. What would be your *need*?" Karras liked challenging his team with nonmanufacturing examples.

Solar System Model

"To keep the medical equipment running accurately, to have no break-downs, and to have critical replacement parts readily available," Dave replied. "And you probably need infection control," said Sophie. "And cost management," Ed added. They continued like that till they had developed the following image, *Equipment Maintenance System in a Hospital*.

Equipment Maintenance System in a Hospital

*Availability is a measure of equipment being ready to run properly whenever it is needed. MTTR stands for mean time to repair; MTBF means mean time between failure.

Karras continued, "Let's look at lean thinking in the same way. Everything starts with the customer. Our business need is to provide the *exact item* required at the *highest quality* at the *lowest cost* in the *shortest lead time*. Lean tools, like value-stream mapping and visual management, are extremely powerful. But they are means to that end—not an end in themselves."

Karras drew out another solar system, *Lean Thinking System.*

"We use the tools that we *need*," Karras said. "No need—no activity. Moreover, the tools are linked to one another. Value-stream mapping helps to *focus* problem-solving; visual management *supports* standardized work. Demand leveling supports just-in-time delivery."

Ed, Sophie, and Dave absorbed this in silence.

"Where's strategy deployment fit in?" Ed asked.

Lean Thinking System

"Think of strategy deployment as our guidance and delivery system, focusing lean tools on our business need. Or you can think of it as a compass that keeps everything aligned with True North."

"I think I now understand why lean tools and serial kaizen events haven't improved our bottom line," Dave said. "It's more than just using tools. They haven't been focused on our business need."

"I call that the 'wheel of fortune' approach," Karras said. "You try tool after tool, with minimal impact, eventually giving up.

"I've also run across the 'Christmas tree syndrome,'" Karras added, "where companies have an annual 'lean audit' done by external auditors. The plant knows what the auditors want to see, so it's like Christmas. They put up a tree, decorate it, and put some presents underneath. When the auditors leave, they take down the tree until next year, and it's business as usual."

Sophie, Ed, and Dave laughed out loud. "Really, John, you're too much," said Sophie.

"Can we do a solar system for our strategy deployment system?" Ed asked.

Through Karras' questioning approach, the team defined its planning and execution need as follows:

- ⊙ *Focus*—we have a shared understanding of our critical few goals.
- ⊙ *Alignment*—our activities are necessary and sufficient and are focused on our common goals.
- ⊙ *Quick response*—we identify problems quickly and fix them.

Then Karras illustrated the components of strategy deployment, *Atlas Industries Solar System*.

"Interesting," said Dave. "I've never seen all the pieces together. I'm sure you'll be explaining what all this means. …"

"You can bet on it, Dave," Karras replied.

Atlas Industries Solar System

Current Condition—Atlas Planning and Execution System

Then they went over to shipping to watch the pallet-making process. Finished-goods inventory towered above them. Karras pointed to the piles. "Sophie, have any of these ever fallen over?" Sophie nodded.

"We need a countermeasure and quickly," Karras said. "Let's keep out of the line of fire."

"To improve," Karras went on, "we need to understand our current planning and execution system. So what's our current condition?"

"We have no strategic plan," said Ed, "and no planning and execution system. All we have is an annual budget planning process."

Nobody argued, not even Dave. Ed had been with Atlas for almost 20 years and knew the plant better than anyone. He and Sophie had put their backs into the plant's lean activities, spending hours on the shopfloor with improvement teams.

"I appreciate your candor," said Karras. "Over the next few weeks, we'll continue our diagnosis."

After their walkthrough, Dave asked to speak with Karras privately.

"John, I'm embarrassed," he said. "The shopfloor is a reflection of *me*. I feel like I've forgotten how to manage. I don't know what to do."

"It takes a big man to say that, Dave," Karras replied. "It's a good sign, too—you know that you don't know. Want to know a secret? I don't know what to do either."

Dave laughed, relieved, and began to grasp Karras' "warm heart" principle: *Hard on the problem—easy on the people.*

Over the next few weeks, the group continued their diagnosis by walking the shop floor; attending team, section, and department meetings; and by reviewing the existing information flows.

Karras kept asking the questions:

- ⊙ What is the current condition in each zone?
- ⊙ Are hot spots visible to everyone?
- ⊙ What are we doing about them?

Information flow, the lifeblood of planning and execution, was a point of focus. They also visited some of Atlas' biggest customers where Karras asked questions like:

- ⊙ How is Atlas Industries viewed in your company?
- ⊙ What are the top three things we can do to improve our products and services?
- ⊙ What technologies do we need to develop to work with you?

Karras called the management team together to summarize what they had found. Nobody knew how their new COO would deal with this formidable list. But Karras just asked a lot of questions. They had an honest, frank discussion about the company's problems:

- ⊙ *Visual management was weak despite the 5S training.* Quality standards for products and processes were invisible. Process layouts were unclear; there were no discernible home positions for tools, parts, or machines. Team boards were used sporadically.

- ⊙ *Information flow was chaotic.* There were dozens of reports, hundreds of charts, but no coherent story.

- ⊙ *Zone control was weak.* In general, team leaders and group leaders did not know their hot spots. Production managers expected functional groups—Quality Assurance, Human Resources, Production Control, and Logistics—to solve quality, safety, absenteeism, and material problems.

- *Plant and departmental meetings were long and dull*. People reported production shortfalls and gave perfunctory explanations. Occasionally, someone would mention a serious safety or machine downtime incident.

- *Problem-solving was sporadic and ineffective*. There was no standard approach; only engineers and specialists were expected to solve problems.

- *There was little evidence of team member involvement*.

- *Customers viewed Atlas Industries as a reliable but not stellar supplier of commodity condensers, heat exchangers, and evaporator coils*. Despite long-standing relationships with Atlas' sales force, customers looked elsewhere for innovation and customization.

- *"It's not enough to provide cool air at low cost,"* an executive at a customer site told them. "It's also got to be clean and healthy air." He seemed anxious about mold spores and other biological allergens, which apparently grew on evaporator coils, heat exchangers, and condensers.

The management team learned an important lesson: It was OK to be honest.

The Big Questions

Describe your organization's current management system. Use the solar system model presented in this chapter if it helps.

How well is your management system understood across the organization? Do you have any examples that support your answer?

Which elements of your management system are effective? Why?

Which elements of your management system are not effective? Why not?

How is your management system taught and communicated across the organization?

How would you begin to improve your organization's management system?

Describe information flow in your organization.

How would you improve information flow?

"So what's our current condition in Quality?" Karras asked.

They were in the QA team room. Charts covered the walls: run, control, pie, and Pareto charts; fishbones, fault trees, and FMEAs.[1]

But nobody could answer Karras' question.

"So which of these charts has meaning?" Karras continued.

The QA director walked around the room with a high-lighter. "This one has meaning," he said, "and this one. Oh, and this one over here."

"Please put the meaningful charts on one piece of paper," said Karras. "Include a target line—a red, green, or yellow indication—and briefly explain what's happening with a text box below each chart."

That makes sense, thought the QA director. The QA team was committed to visual management. But many of the wall charts were out of date. Did anyone read them?

"Please don't misunderstand," Karras told them. "Wall charts are OK so long as they answer the main questions."

"What are your hot spots?" thought the QA director. "And what are you doing about them?"

Chapter 4
Understanding Our Mess

"We need to understand our mess," said their COO. "That's not being negative. Life is messy."

It was a cold December morning. The entire management team, including Harman, was in the final-assembly team room. A few of the directors, like Phil Lucas of HR and Jim Torrey of Sales and Marketing, had had a hard time finding it. It was loud in there. Through the glass they could see material handlers rushing parts to the line.

Karras began by giving them an overview of the strategy deployment system. He explained that it comprised six steps:

1. Define True North—Atlas Industries' strategic and philosophical purpose.

2. Develop the plan.

3. Deploy the plan.

4. Monitor the plan.

5. Solve problems.

6. Improve the system.

Elements two, three, four and five, he explained, correspond to the *Plan-Do-Check-Adjust* cycle, also known as the scientific method.

---

1. Fishbones, fault trees, and FMEAs (failure mode and effects analysis) are all analytical tools. For more information, see: Michael Brassard and Diane Ritter, *The Memory Jogger, A Pocket Guide of Tools for Continuous Improvement and Effective Planning* (Methuen, MA, GOAL/APC, 1994).

He explained that the leader's job was to *practice and teach PDCA*. Step six reflected the messiness of the world, where little went according to plan, and so the strategy deployment system must be ongoing. Management was a game without end. The challenge was to get better each day.

Karras then explained that they needed to create a *tree* of activities with "True North," Atlas Industries' business purpose, at the top. Everything had to flow or *branch* from this and be connected to everything else—as well as aligned with True North.

"True North comprises a hard business goal and a broad brush goal," said Karras, going to the whiteboard. "Here are our hard business goals for next year: Revenue of $252 million, EBIT of 5%, and a cash-flow increase of $10 million. This year's revenue and EBIT will be about $247 million and 1.4%, respectively."

"Bill Harman, Ed, and I came up with these goals," Karras said. "What do you think?"

Atlas Business Goals

What is our purpose?
To make money

_____

Targets:
Revenue = $252 million
EBIT = 5%
Cash-flow increase = $10 million

True North

If we don't know where we're going, we'll never get there. "True North" expresses business needs that *must* be achieved and exerts a magnetic *pull*. True North is a contract, a bond, and not merely a wish list. For Atlas Industries, True North means, above all, stopping the hemorrhage in revenues and achieving a healthy level of profitability. That is not to say other needs will be ignored, only that business needs form a changing hierarchy.

For companies whose condition is less dire, True North can be expressed in a more balanced manner. At Toyota, for example, True North usually comprises something for the company and its shareholders, customers, team members, and the community:

- *Company and its shareholders*: revenue, return on sales, market share, and margins.

- *Customers*: in-plant and in-service quality, warranty costs, and quality awards.

- *Team members*: safety, ergonomics, good working conditions, training and development opportunities, and employment stability.

- *Community*: environmental leadership, involvement in communities, and stable employment.

This way of thinking is reflected in the "balanced scorecard" concept. Ignoring it can cripple or kill an enterprise. For example, manufacturers that ignore safety may face crippling liabilities caused by occupational hazards. Mining companies that ignore the environment can face cleanup costs that dwarf their assets. And companies that ignore team member morale will find it difficult to sustain continuous improvement.

"Well, given that we've lost Henderson Controls, a $12 million account," said Dave, "I'd say they're aggressive."

"These numbers *must* be achieved," Harman said. "We have to get out of the commodity trap, and we have to be self-funding."

"Why are we including cash flow?" Sophie asked. "We've always focused on EBIT."

"Good question, Sophie," Karras replied. "Ed, would you like to explain?"

"Standard cost accounting isn't the best scoreboard," Ed told them. "I've always known this but never admitted it until John challenged me. EBIT and other standard profit measures can be misleading. For example, we know that lean thinking is about reducing waste, and that excess inventory is the mother of all waste. So reducing inventory is an important long-term goal. But initially, this will *negatively* affect EBIT."

"You've got to be *kidding*," said Vic Falcone, aluminum-fin fabrication manager. "What kind of scoreboard is that?"

"Right or wrong, that's how we have to report to regulators, stakeholders, and potential investors. But that doesn't mean we have to manage our business that way," Ed replied. "We want to use *real* numbers, which is why we've included cash flow. If we do this right, we'll free up a lot of cash. EBIT improvement eventually will follow. One of my personal goals this year will be to simplify our accounting system and financial reports. It's a big job."

"Ed and John spent a lot of time explaining it to me," Harman said. "It makes sense."

"Any other hard business goals we can think of?" Karras asked the team.

"Well, we don't want to get fired," said Jose Cano, tube-and-header fabrication manager.

"Yeah," said Bob Green of tube-and-fin brazing and assembly, "and we don't want our people to lose their jobs either. The past few years, our town has had a hard time."

"Let's call it stable employment with a target of no layoffs," said Sophie.

Karras nodded. "Lean thinking is about eliminating waste—not people. Our people know where the waste is. If we involve them, they'll help eliminate it—but only if we're committed to employment stability. We're lucky to have an owner that gets it." Harman shrugged.

"Okay," Karras said, "we've got our end-of-pipe metrics."[2]

Atlas Business Goals

What is our purpose?
To make money
Employment stability

Targets:
Revenue = $252 million
EBIT = 5%
Cash-flow increase = $10 million
No layoffs

2. Metrics indicative of performance outcomes.

Employment Stability

The "no layoffs" goal is essential. Would team members help us improve if doing so put jobs at risk? If instead team members that could be released are redirected to help grow and improve the business, a benevolent cycle can develop: Involvement creates improvement, improvement creates involvement, etc.

Can you commit to no layoffs if you're facing a financial crisis? Probably not; however, you might take the following approach: be honest, be fair, and downsize selectively. Being honest means saying, "Look, either we save some of the jobs or none of the jobs." After you've made the painful, necessary cuts, *commit to employment stability*. Being fair is self-explanatory. Downsizing selectively means keeping the people you need to grow the business. Avoid offering buy-out packages to all employees, because your best people might take them.

True North: *Speed—Cost—Innovation*

"Now we need to define our *broad-brush* goal," Karras told them, "a short phrase which expresses our vision, direction and will. The Japanese would call it our *hoshin*. It's not just a marketing slogan. We need to feel it in our *guts*. Who are we? What do we believe in? Where are we going? What have we learned? Reflection point: What has Henderson Controls taught us?"

The management team had an intense, emotional discussion. Karras pushed them hard. "What would failure mean for our community, our team members, and our own families? What do our customers *really* want? What advantages do we have over our competitors? What do we have to do to compete with them?"

There were several shouting matches, as long-buried emotions, frustrations, and fears came to the surface. Gradually, the body language changed; stiff, defensive postures opened up; people got up, walked around, and began speaking with their whole bodies. Eventually, the team agreed upon the hoshin: *Speed—Cost—Innovation*, which reflected their consensus on the following points:

- ⊙ If we continue to make commodities, we're *toast* because we can't compete on labor cost alone.

- ⊙ We're close to our customers, and should be able to deliver products quicker.

- ⊙ We need to innovate. What do our customers really want or need? We have longstanding relationships; we need to translate them into great products.

Atlas Business Goals

Speed—Cost—Innovation

Targets:

Revenue = $252 million

EBIT = 5%

Cash-flow increase = $10 million

No layoffs

Straight from the Gut

Speed, cost, and innovation—what's the big deal? The mission statements of many companies cite these words. The difference is that the Atlas management team arrived at them viscerally, through deeply felt emotion and experience.

A good hoshin makes an emotional impact and creates a sense of excitement. It isn't just a marketing slogan. Memorable Toyota hoshins like *Internationalize* or *Beloved Company*, although difficult to comprehend by outsiders, conveyed great meaning to team members.

Leadership is about language. Out of the chaos—events, rumors, data, impressions—the leader needs to create meaning. Base your hoshin on visceral experience; go to the gemba, look around, and talk to people.

Each organization needs to answer this question for itself. SQDC works well in many organizations, but may not be precisely right for yours. It's easy to see how business fundamentals can be quite different for a service or retail organization vs. that of a manufacturer. Other possible expressions include development or innovation (entailing R&D and new product development), productivity, supply chain, and people (entailing safety, morale, and skill development).

The important thing is to think through and chart your own course, as the Atlas team is trying to do, and to pick metrics that people understand. Please minimize the obscure financial ratios that litter so many corporate reports.

Second Level of Planning and Execution Tree

Then they developed the second level of their planning and execution tree. Like a tree, Atlas' goals continue to branch out through the organization. Karras explained that this second level of branching could either address *functional* strategies or strategies around what he called *business fundamentals*.

Karras said that at Toyota factories, planning was typically organized around their business fundamentals: *Safety*, *Quality*, *Delivery*, and *Cost*—or SQDC. Karras recommended that Atlas organize accordingly, and there was broad agreement. "But do *Safety*, *Quality*, *Delivery*, and *Cost* adequately express our business fundamentals?" he asked.

After a long question-and-answer session, the team's consensus was SQDC didn't quite fit Atlas Industries' business situation. *Employee Satisfaction*, *Customer Satisfaction*, *Delivery*, and *Profitability* were a better fit.

⊙ *Employee Satisfaction*: health and safety, and morale;

⊙ *Customer Satisfaction*: incoming, in-plant, and outgoing quality;

⊙ *Delivery*: incoming, outgoing, and in-plant logistics and building to customer demand; and

⊙ *Profitability*: a combination of revenue (comprising New Product Development, and Sales and Marketing), cost management, and cost reduction.

"You're learning an important lesson," Karras said. "We need to tailor the system to fit our needs."

Second Level of Tree at Atlas Industries

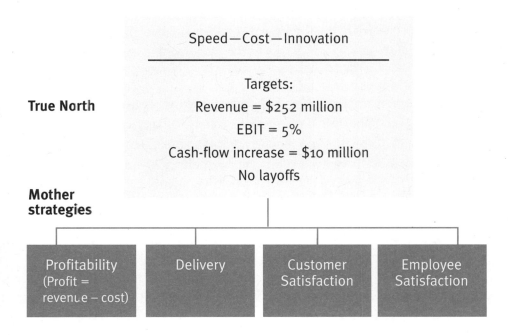

True North

Speed—Cost—Innovation

Targets:
Revenue = $252 million
EBIT = 5%
Cash-flow increase = $10 million
No layoffs

Mother strategies

| Profitability (Profit = revenue – cost) | Delivery | Customer Satisfaction | Employee Satisfaction |

"Let's see if I understand this, John," said Dave. "Does each director have to write a strategy for *Profitability, Delivery, Customer Satisfaction,* and *Employee Satisfaction*?"

After another question-and-answer series the team learned that:

- Directors must translate "mother" strategies into meaningful tactics. In large departments like Manufacturing, this might mean "baby" strategies corresponding to each mother strategy (e.g., one for *Profitability, Delivery*, etc.). Smaller departments, like Finance, might have a single baby strategy that addressed all the mother strategies.

- Directors should only address items *critical to their zones*. "It's all about focus," Karras said. "What three or four things will you emphasize?"

- Critical items will probably require baby strategies. For example, the *Profitability* strategy would surely address New Product Development, Sales and Marketing, and cost reductions.

Business Fundamentals vs. Functional Strategies

This is an important decision point. The second level of the tree largely determines the structure of the planning and execution system.

Structuring by Business Fundamentals: Structuring based on business fundamentals—for example, Safety, Quality, Delivery, and Cost (SQDC), as is common in Toyota factories—compels cross-functionality and is usually the most effective approach. "Mother" strategies for each business fundamental support True North, and each function develops support or "baby" strategies in alignment with the mother strategies. For example, Manufacturing might have a baby strategy for Cost, one for Quality, etc.

Structuring by Function: In large organizations with multiple divisions, it often makes sense to structure the second level of the tree according to function. This engages functional groups by requiring them to write their own mother strategies. For example, each division would develop a mother A3 aligned with True North and reflecting the realities in their division (their zone). Deployment within divisions would then proceed according to business fundamentals, as described above.

Where functions commonly work together and are naturally focused on and rally around a True North, structuring by function can work well. However, the risk of this approach is the gradual emergence of departmental silos and planning in isolation, with each function progressively more worried about executing its own mother strategy (even to the detriment of other functions) rather than really supporting True North and the company as a whole.

Each company should tailor the tree to its business need, culture, and fit. There is no one best way.

Karras then asked for current *process metrics* corresponding to the second level of the tree. He asked Dave to facilitate the discussion. It turns out that there was plenty of data, but comparatively little meaning. Important measures like first-time-through quality and new-product-launch data were missing or unreliable. Core activities like cost reduction and the suggestion program had been abandoned. Eventually, the team came up with the following process metrics, which were both reliable and available:

Second Level of Tree at Atlas Industries with Current Process Metrics

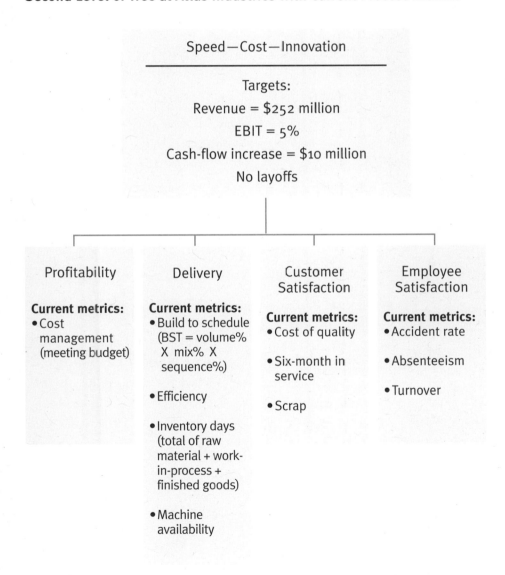

Speed — Cost — Innovation

Targets:
Revenue = $252 million
EBIT = 5%
Cash-flow increase = $10 million
No layoffs

Profitability

Current metrics:
• Cost management (meeting budget)

Delivery

Current metrics:
• Build to schedule (BST = volume% X mix% X sequence%)

• Efficiency

• Inventory days (total of raw material + work-in-process + finished goods)

• Machine availability

Customer Satisfaction

Current metrics:
• Cost of quality

• Six-month in service

• Scrap

Employee Satisfaction

Current metrics:
• Accident rate

• Absenteeism

• Turnover

The purpose of rating systems is to help tell the story so that there is a shared understanding of what's important. Reasonable people provided with reasonable information will make reasonable decisions. Simple definitions—such as green (meets target), yellow (off target), and red (way off target)—are preferable to hair-splitting distinctions that can lead to game-playing.

Effective rating systems help you decide what to talk about, so use terminology that is easily understood within your organization. The goal of rating systems is discovery, discussion, and problem-solving.

"Do these metrics adequately reflect *Speed—Cost—Innovation?*" Karras asked. "And if not, what's missing?"

"We're missing *Speed* and *Innovation*," Dave said. The others agreed.

Dave led the team through more brainstorming, with a focus on New Product Development, supply chain, and team member involvement. Here's what they came up with, *Second Level of Tree with Current and Needed Metrics.*

....

"That's enough for today," Karras said. "Good work, and here's your next assignment. What is our current condition in *Profitability, Delivery, Customer Satisfaction,* and *Employee Satisfaction?* Let's break up into four groups. Tell the story using as few charts as possible. Rate each chart green (meets target), yellow (off target), or red (way off target). Confirm by going to the shopfloor."

"But we don't have targets for a lot of this stuff," Bob Jonas, the QA director, said.

"Where we lack a target, make an estimate," Karras replied. "We can refine it as we learn more. Key point: please make all our problems visible."

Second Level of Tree with Current and Needed Metrics

Speed—Cost—Innovation

Targets:

Revenue = $252 million

EBIT = 5%

Cash-flow increase = $10 million

No layoffs

Profitability	Delivery	Customer Satisfaction	Employee Satisfaction
Current metrics: • Cost management (meeting budget) **Needed metrics:** • Cost reduction ($ per unit) • New product launches (throughput, lead time, engineering change orders, and utilization rates)	**Current metrics:** • Build to schedule (BST = volume% X mix% X sequence%) • Efficiency • Inventory days (total of raw material + work-in-process + finished goods) • Machine availability **Needed metrics:** • Total lead time • Total logistics cost • Inventory days (raw material, work-in-process, and finished goods) • In-plant part-outs (number, related production loss)	**Current metrics:** • Cost of quality • Six-month in service • Scrap **Needed metrics:** • First time through (overall and by department) • Defects per unit	**Current metrics:** • Accident rate • Absenteeism • Turnover **Needed metrics:** • Suggestion program data (ideas implemented, cost and other improvements)

Year-to-Date Results—Atlas Business Fundamentals

A week later, here is what the teams presented.

Delivery

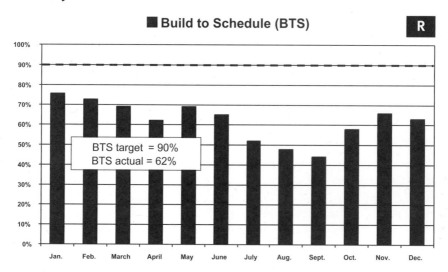

BTS = Volume % X Mix % X Sequence %. BTS reflects ability to meet the production schedule.

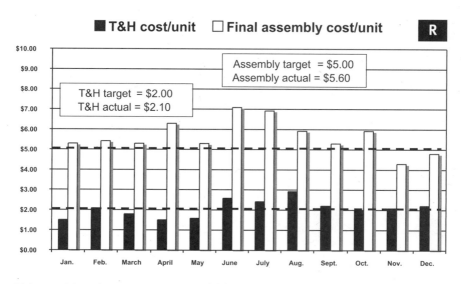

Tube-and-header cost-per-unit and final assembly cost-per-unit are good measures of production efficiency.

Delivery (continued)

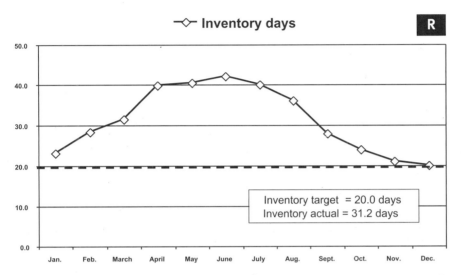

Inventory days   R

Inventory target = 20.0 days
Inventory actual = 31.2 days

As a rule, the more inventory a factory needs to sustain throughput, the less capable it is. World-class factories run lean. Less-capable factories buffer their problems (e.g., quality, machine breakdowns, and absenteeism) with inventory. Excess inventory swells operating expense and shrinks profitability. Atlas Industries tracks the total of raw material, work-in-process, and finished-goods inventory.

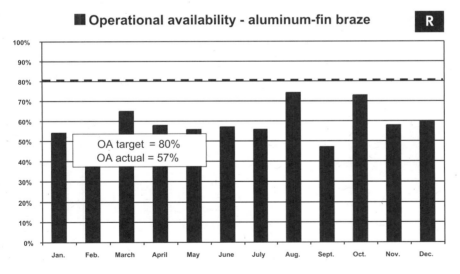

■ Operational availability - aluminum-fin braze   R

OA target = 80%
OA actual = 57%

Operational availability (OA) = (Operating time required – Downtime) divided by Operating time required. Downtime includes machine breakdowns, changeovers, and maintenance work. Availability reflects the likelihood that a piece of equipment will run properly when it is needed.

Customer Satisfaction

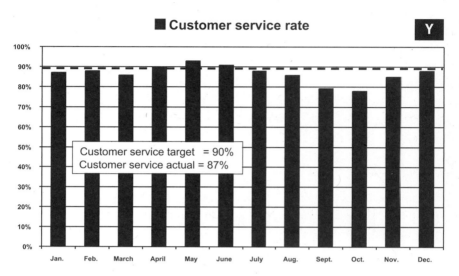

■ Customer service rate **Y**

Customer service target = 90%
Customer service actual = 87%

The customer service rate is the rate at which the customer receives the right part, in the right quantity, and at the right time. Instability in the factory or supply chain degrades customer service rates. Instability is usually buffered by expanding finished-goods inventories and by expediting delivery, at the expense of profitability.

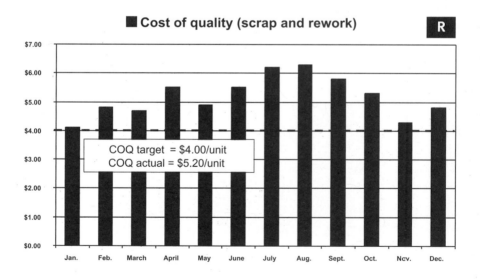

■ Cost of quality (scrap and rework) **R**

COQ target = $4.00/unit
COQ actual = $5.20/unit

The customer satisfaction charts suggested that Atlas had problems with process capability and containment. "Not only do you make junk," Karras observed, "but you also ship it." Karras pushed the team: "Why did build-to-schedule drop during the summer months? Why did cost of quality and inventory spike? Who can connect the dots?"

Profitability

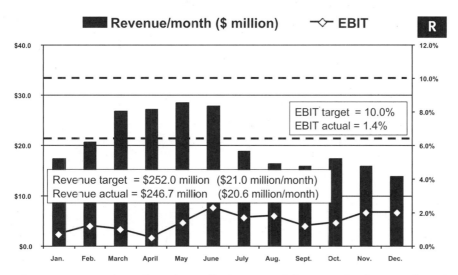

The revenue results reflect the cyclical nature of the HVAC business. Atlas sold more condensers and evaporators coils in the spring when its customers anticipated summer demand. The absence of level demand strained the production system. OEM business was cyclical, mirroring residential construction. Wholesaler demand, driven by coil replacement in existing systems, was less cyclical.

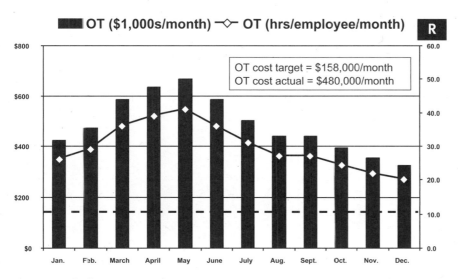

Overtime (OT) was a big problem. Atlas came close to meeting its revenue targets, but wasn't making any money. "Inventory, scrap, and overtime are killing us," said Ed Wolf.

Employee Satisfaction

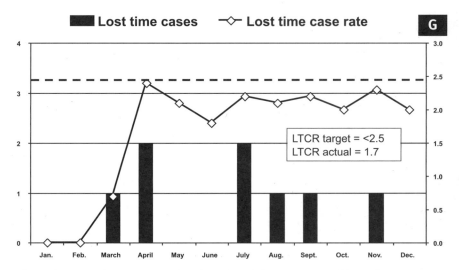

The safety results, expressed as lost time injury cases and lost time case rate (LTCR), were the only green results for Atlas.

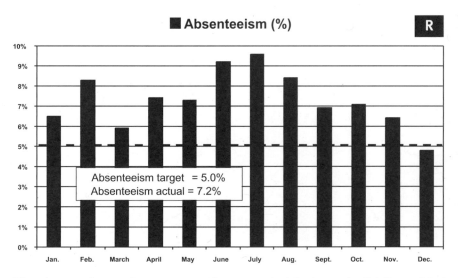

The absenteeism and turnover results suggested that people didn't want to be at the plant.

The management team was glum after the report-out. "I knew we were screwed up," said Sophie. "But not *that* screwed up."

"One lousy green chart, what a disaster," said the QA director. Deb Kramer, Carrie Webb, and Jim Torrey were quiet, aware of the metrics gap in their respective departments.

"Better polish the resume," said Phil Lucas, HR director.

Karras was unperturbed. He passed out a one-page "dashboard," which Ed and he had put together (*see next page*).

"Over time, this dashboard will evolve into our main checking tool," Karras told them.

"We still don't understand what's happening in New Product Development, Sales and Marketing, or our supply chain," Karras cautioned. "We'll work on that. But we're beginning to grasp the situation in our factory. Can anyone explain the mess?"

Blank stares all around.

Value-Stream Maps and Dashboards

Value-stream maps and dashboards are complementary tools. Value-stream maps help answer the critical questions that arise during the *Plan* phase of the Plan-Do-Check-Adjust (PDCA) cycle:

⊙ Where are we now?

⊙ Where do we need to go?

⊙ What are the obstacles in our path?

Dashboards are real-time management tools that help the zone leader *Check* and *Adjust* the plan. They are also an expression of zone control: "Here is what happened during my watch, and what I'm doing about it."

Understanding Our Mess—Karras' Hypothesis

"Let me suggest an explanation," Karras continued. "Instability in the four Ms—man/woman, machine, method, and materials—is degrading our production system. That's why our lean activities haven't taken root. You can't flow or pull unless you have stable machines, manpower, and processes. And we're buffering the instability with inventory, overtime, and expediting."

The directors were silent. "The truth at last," said Dave.

Karras shrugged. "I might be wrong, you know."

"Man, I wish you were," Vic Falcone said. "We firefight like crazy. I'm drained at the end of the day."

"I want *each of you* to make and test hypotheses, Karras told them. "Let's accept mine for now. What are the implications for the coming year's strategy?"

"It means that next year we should focus on stability," Sophie suggested.

Karras nodded. "Value-stream mapping, visual management, standardized work, pull systems—you've done all the right things. But they weren't sustained because of instability in the 4Ms."

"We can use our value-stream maps to focus," Dave said, "and lean tools to stabilize."

Karras nodded again. "You'll notice that each chart on our dashboard has a text box beneath it—and that each text box is blank. Here's your next assignment. Please identify our hot spots and possible countermeasures. Go to the shopfloor; use your value-stream maps."

The management team members were beginning to understand their business need and the "mess" in the factory. Now they had to do something about it.

The View from Above

Harman and Karras met at the Imperial Bar & Grill to discuss the Atlas team's progress.

"I hear that you're pushing the team hard, John," said Harman. "I like that."

"Got to," Karras replied.

"I also like how we've defined True North."

Karras nodded. "We have to make an emotional connection with people. Strategy isn't just about numbers—it's about what's in your guts and heart."

"What's your assessment?" Harman asked.

"The team is too dependent on me, which is normal at this stage," Karras said. "But I'm going to start stepping back. We need to grow more leaders."

"Is that why you keep challenging them with questions?"

"You bet; I don't want to *tell* them what to do. My Japanese mentor used to say, 'We're not just building cars, we're building *people*.'"

Harman smiled. "You can give a man a fish, or ..."

"Time for a drink," said Karras.

The View from the Floor

Tom Schmidt was a veteran team leader in tube-and-header fabrication. He was widely respected for his manufacturing experience and for the way he treated people. Karras liked him; they often had lunch together at the picnic tables near the line.

"I don't really see a difference, John," Tom said, "except that you're out here quite a bit. We're also beginning to see the directors on the floor. To be honest, they're a nuisance. They don't know what they're seeing or what they're looking for."

"Thanks," Karras said. "I'll check in with you from time to time. Please keep me honest."

The Big Questions

What is your organization's purpose?

Does your organization have a planning and execution tree? If so, describe it. If not, what would be in the first and second levels?

What are your organization's end-of-pipe (downstream) targets?

What are your organization's process (upstream) targets?

What are your organization's three biggest problems?

What is the view from the floor at your company?

Plan-Do-Check-Adjust—Our Foundation

The Scientific Method

The *Plan-Do-Check-Adjust* (PDCA) cycle is W. Edwards Deming's gift to the world. No mental model is more important—and more misunderstood. PDCA is an expression of the scientific method to which our society owes its prosperity. It's also the foundation of strategy deployment.

Grasping the Situation

The precursor to PDCA, and what Atlas Industries has been doing to this point, is grasping the situation (GTS), which entails asking questions such as:

⊙ What is actually happening?
⊙ What should be happening?
⊙ What must be happening?
⊙ What is the ideal condition?

GTS means grasping the where, what, and why of abnormalities by scanning a mile wide and inch deep to spot an abnormality, and an inch wide and mile deep to understand the root cause of the abnormality.

We can only do this by going to the gemba to see what's actually happening. Then we reflect and figure out what it means. As Karras explained to the Atlas team, effective leaders move fluidly between the world of experience and the world of thought. Because GTS supports each phase of PDCA, we place it in the center.

Plan represents our *hypothesis*. In the context of standardized work, it means, "If we carry out these set of steps, we believe we will achieve these safety, quality, delivery, and cost results." In the context of strategic planning, it means, "If we take these actions over this time, we will achieve the required result."

Grasp the Situation at the Center of PDCA

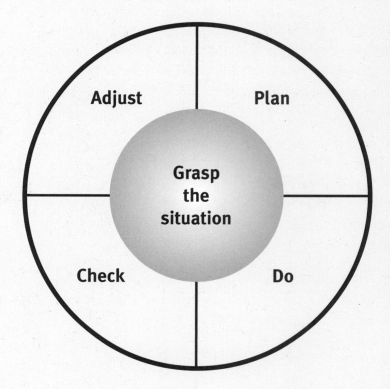

Through our plan, therefore, we answer the core planning questions:

- ⊙ Where are we going?
- ⊙ How do we get there?

During the *Plan* phase we must also develop SMART metrics (simple, measurable, achievable, reasonable, and trackable) for both the end-of-pipe (i.e., the outcome) and the process.

Mini-PDCA within Do

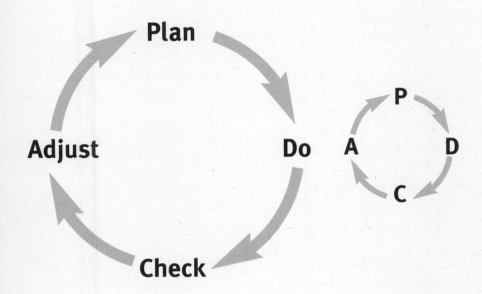

Do is our experiment and entails:

⊙ Translating or deploying our goals and activities level by level, and
⊙ Carrying out the corresponding action plans.

It's wise to *pilot* major activities before full implementation. The learning gained strengthens our plan. Thus, we include a mini-PDCA loop within the Do phase.

Check entails observing and assessing results against the targets set in the *Plan* phase. Most businesses neither respect nor reward good checkers. Yet PDCA most often stumbles here. At companies like Toyota, "How will you check?" is a mantra.

Good checking means answering questions like:

- ⊙ What will I check?
- ⊙ How will I check?
- ⊙ Who will I check?
- ⊙ How often will I check?
- ⊙ Where and when will I check?
- ⊙ What am I likely to find, and what will I do about it?

Good checking means going to the *gemba*, the place where stuff happens. The gemba can be the shopfloor, sales office, service center, supplier loading dock, operating room, or banking center. Check also means developing robust check processes at the company, plant, department, section, and team level—and then linking them, like a series of gears.

Adjust means reflecting on the results of checking. If the results meet our targets, standardize! Our hypothesis has been confirmed. If not, we must adjust our hypothesis to fit the facts, which usually means problem-solving. *Adjust*, like *Check*, has a lowly position in traditional management philosophy. The word implies some minor tweaking. Yet *Adjust* might be the most challenging PDCA phase. It requires following an often-complex thread of causality from the so-called "point of cause" (the actual location and moment the abnormality occurs) to the "root cause," which is usually remote in time and space.

Problem-solving is detective work. Our management challenge is to create *problem-solvers* by restoring its mystique and by teaching a simple, robust problem-solving approach that everyone can use. Contemporary problem-solving approaches are often too complex for the best sleuths—our team members and supervisors.

PDCA Creates a Community of Scientists

In a *Harvard Business Review* article,[2] Steven Spears and Kent Bowen postulated that the "Toyota Production System creates a community of scientists." Indeed, the scientific method, expressed as PDCA, is the engine of most great companies. The top half of the diagram below illustrates different management activities, ranging from the high-level and transcending into the organization. The bottom half shows the corresponding tools with those management activities. For example, A3s are a tool used in activity planning.

PDCA at Lean Organizations

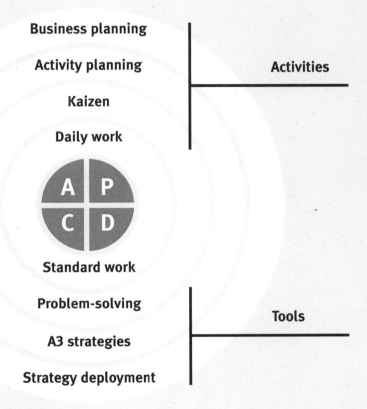

Business planning

Activity planning   Activities

Kaizen

Daily work

A | P
C | D

Standard work

Problem-solving   Tools

A3 strategies

Strategy deployment

2. Steven Spears and Kent Bowen, "Decoding the DNA of the Toyota Production System," *Harvard Business Review*, October/November 1999.

"If you can't express your plan on one page," said Karras, "you probably don't understand it."

"Yeah but ...," said the director.

"A picture is worth a thousand words."

"But ..."

"Complexity is a crude state," Karras continued. "Simplicity marks the end of a process of refining."

"Yeah, but ..."

"Let's take it from the top," Karras said.

Chapter 5
Plan—Telling Persuasive Stories

'Back to School'

Christmas came and went, and a snowstorm ushered in the New Year. The Atlas Industries team was beginning to understand its hot spots. Karras had declared a moratorium on needless meetings and e-mail. He arranged for regular gemba sessions to be held every Tuesday and Thursday in a different department. They'd begin with a review of an element of strategy deployment followed by a shopfloor process review, at which the department leader presented a current improvement activity. "Over time, I want each of you to start teaching," Karras told them.

Karras had given Christmas gifts to each function: electronic whiteboards, flipcharts, and microphones. The Atlas team would spend much of the coming year studying Karras' copious whiteboard notes. He had also given the directors a list of references to study. "We're all going back to school," he said.

At their first gemba session, in the aluminum-fin-fabrication team room, Karras began by asking, "What is a *plan*?"

"A plan tells us where we're going," said Ed Wolf, "and how we get there."

Karras nodded. "*Where are we going? And how do we get there?* The critical planning questions! Does a plan have any other purpose?"

They mulled it over. "Our plan tells us whether we're on course," offered Bob Green.

"And when we're *off* course," Sophie Suarez added.

"Correct." Karras said. "Our plan makes abnormalities visible so we can respond quickly. Not much goes 'according to plan.'"

"Do you have a concrete example of your approach to planning?" Phil Lucas asked. "We had some training a few years ago. It wasn't very practical."

"Suppose a guy wanted to become a good golfer," Karras replied, "as a way of reducing stress. Let's start by developing a tree diagram. We'll use a simple brainstorming tool called a *mind map*. You can also use other tools, like affinity charts. Key point: Involve your team members; ask a lot of questions."

Karras led them through his example on the whiteboard, getting them to contribute ideas on how to become a good golfer. They had fun with it, making up stuff as they went along. Here is the preliminary mind map of ideas that might help a person achieve the golf objective.

Becoming a Good Golfer—Ideas

Objectives: To have fun. To reduce stress.
Targets: To shoot in the 90s (average) by June 30.
To reduce stress-test score to target zone by Sept 30.

Delegate work

Free up time   Get enough rest   Buy new putter

Talk to family

Prepare physically   Buy putting practice mat

Talk to business partners

Find a good teacher   Get right equipment

Find local driving range

Find right golf course   Read Jack Nicklaus biography

Have golf swing analyzed

Read about mental aspects of golf

Meditate 20 minutes each day   Work on flexibility and strength at gym

Subscribe to *Golf Channel*

Then they grouped the ideas and gave each grouping a short, action title. This was their tree diagram:

Becoming a Good Golfer—Tree Diagram

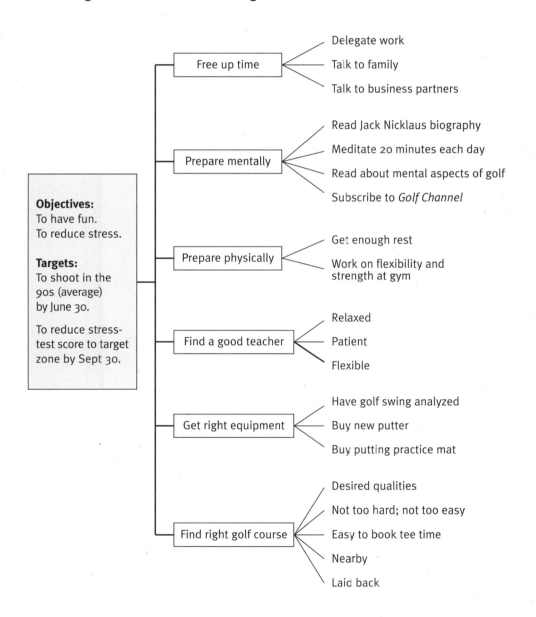

Telling Stories with A3s

Some people may look at an A3 and think it's "too complicated" or "too busy"—a normal reaction to a detailed A3. We're condensing a lot into a small space. But you'll find that good A3 stories have an intuitive flow and can be told in five to 10 minutes. The author tells the story, we follow along on the paper until he or she finishes, and a question-and-answer session follows.

By the time the A3 is presented to senior management, everybody in the room has already seen and agreed to it. At companies like Toyota it's not unusual for an immediate decision to be made after a five-minute presentation.

There is a danger that A3s can be appealing to people short of time and overwhelmed with paper and electronic reports. One piece of paper looks pretty good, and the A3 becomes a dictate from management, a shiny new toy that everyone must use. "From now on, everything will be A3!"

Additionally, people often try to outdo one another by creating fancy graphics or by condensing more and more information on the page. Please remember the purpose of A3s is to gain a shared understanding of a critical issue in order to solve problems and get results.

"Now we can write the better golfer's strategic plan," Karras said. "The most important thing is to tell a clear, concise story on *one page*. My previous company was a supplier to Toyota, and Toyota taught us how to use A3s—a one-page storyboard on 11-inch by 17-inch paper, commonly known as A3-size paper. Logic flows from the top left to the bottom right, and each box leads to the next one. Here's an A3 template with some tips."

A3 Intuitive Flow

Strategy A3 Theme	
• What strategic objectives do we need to achieve this year? • How did we do last year? • What's our history?	• What's our action plan to achieve these objectives (who, what, when, where, and how)?
• What did we do last year? • What worked and didn't work? • What have we learned?	
• What do we need to do to achieve this year's strategic objectives? • How will these actions benefit us?	• Are there any unresolved issues? • Do you need any help with anything? • Anything bothering you?

Focus: ─⟨ e.g., Profitability ⟩   # A3 Theme

Performance, gaps, and targets

Show last year's results. Were we red, yellow, or green?

What's our history? Are we getting better or worse?

Tell the story with a chart, if possible. Minimize words.

What's our year-end target for this coming year and for three to five years out?

Reflection on last year's activities

Assess each of last year's activities: target and actual. Please explain!

What worked and what didn't work? What did we learn?

Rationale for this year's activities

Reflect on what happened last year. What's it mean for this year?

Any new factors to consider (e.g., changes in business environment)?

So, what do we need to do in the coming year?

We can't do everything. Pick three or four areas of emphasis.

How will these activities benefit us?

Signatures: ─⟨ **Sign it and insist your colleagues do the same. Signing means, "I support this plan and will hold up my end."** ⟩

his year's action plan (milestone chart)

ell us the who, what, where, when, and how of your strategy.

rovide SMART (simple, measurable, achievable, reasonable, and trackable) upstream r process goals so we know how we're doing.

ule of thumb: No more than five main actions.

emember, you'll be deploying your plan to your team members.

you put too much in it, the planning tree may turn into a mangrove, and little will get done.

his paper is not a rebinning of everything your department does.

shows what you'll emphasize in order to achieve your strategic goals.

Followup / Unresolved Issues

How will you check what's happening? How will you report?

Anything else bothering you?

Any unresolved issues, question marks, or support needed?

What do you intend to do about them?

Revise your paper based on feedback. It's part of gaining alignment and keeping everyone on the same page.

Author:
Version and date:

When the group reconvened for the next gemba session, Karras presented the strategy, *Becoming a Good Golfer A3*.

The management team reviewed the *Becoming a Good Golfer A3* in silence. It was clear and concise; but Atlas' business was so much more complicated than trying to become a good golfer. Could they write such concise plans that addressed their business needs?

"If you remember just one thing about the A3," said Karras, "let it be this: *It's not about the form.* The A3 template I showed you last time worked well at my last company. But we can change it to suit us. It's a way of thinking. *If I had to tell a complex story on one page, what would I include?*"

Karras then showed them a diagram that further illustrated the A3 thinking process: "The Japanese call it 'thinking way.' Notice that it includes both analysis (number-crunching) and synthesis (storytelling). Here's the acid test: *Is the story persuasive?* In other words, does it make sense? Is it interesting, engaging? Does it make you want to get involved? Could it make you act in ways you otherwise wouldn't act?"

A3 Thinking Process

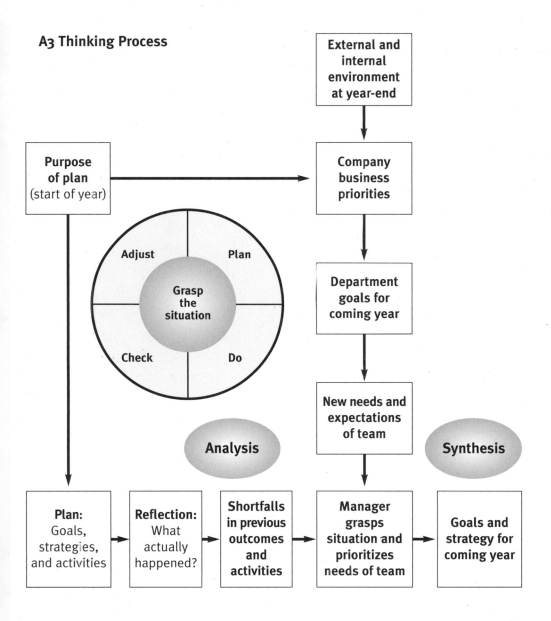

What If You Have a Business-Planning Process?

Strategy deployment doesn't require blowing up your existing planning process and starting anew. Rather, it should complement existing systems. Over time, as your understanding deepens, your existing process will adopt the elements of strategy deployment, in accord with your company's culture and business need.

If your current process is, in effect, a budgeting process, structure your annual strategy deployment cycle to complement it. Start by drawing out the budgeting and strategic planning cycles side-by-side. Then identify obvious difficulties. For example, you may be required to present your budget to the head office *before* you've developed the annual strategy. This can result in the budget driving the strategy, rather than the budget serving the strategy. Develop countermeasures that rationalize the two cycles.

Most problems of synchronization usually occur in the first year. Some companies create a provisional budget category to cover any major capital expenses that come from strategy-deployment-based plans. Other companies use a zero-sum approach: when strategy-deployment-based initiatives run into budgeted operational items, the former prevail—it being understood that strategy deployment supports the year's most important objectives.

Atlas Industries SWOT Analysis

"Now we're ready to look at the big picture," Karras said at the next learning session. "Over the past few months, I've conducted my so-called 'presidential diagnosis.' I've spent a great deal of time with each you; we've gone to the shop floor together and visited our customers and suppliers. We have a dashboard now that shows our current condition on one page. Good work!

"But to develop meaningful strategies for *Profitability*, *Delivery*, etc., we need a broad vision of Atlas. Silo management fosters myopia; we need to get beyond our silos and grasp the entire external and internal environment. Everything is connected. There are a number of available tools that can help us with this. I've found that SWOT analysis (strengths, weaknesses, opportunities, and threats) is as good as any. SWOT can help us to begin to see the whole. As we stabilize, we'll look to value-stream thinking to reinforce the big picture perspective.[1]

"Remember our True North discussion? I want the same kind of intensity and honesty. We need utter candor or we'll never get to what's important. I want to know, *what's our story*? *How did we get into this predicament*? Ed, would you please facilitate our discussion, and drive to the internal and external conditions that affect us?"

Ed led another emotional, freewheeling discussion that addressed the strengths, weaknesses, opportunities, and threats at Atlas. The group produced the following mind map (*see next page*).

Karras was pleased; they were being honest. "Does our theme of *Speed—Cost—Innovation* align with our SWOT analysis?" he asked. Heads nodded.

1. James Womack and Daniel Jones, *Seeing the Whole*, (Cambridge, MA, Lean Enterprise Institute, 2002).

Atlas Industries SWOT Analysis

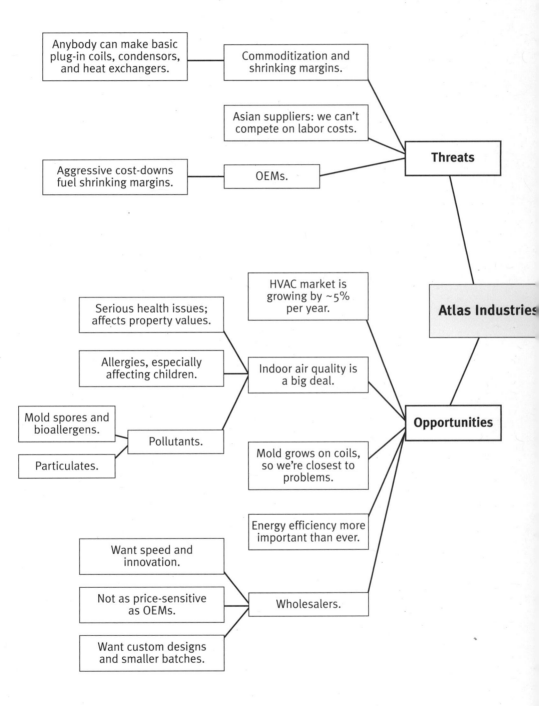

Anybody can make basic plug-in coils, condensors, and heat exchangers.

Commoditization and shrinking margins.

Asian suppliers: we can't compete on labor costs.

Aggressive cost-downs fuel shrinking margins.

OEMs.

Threats

Atlas Industries

HVAC market is growing by ~5% per year.

Serious health issues; affects property values.

Allergies, especially affecting children.

Indoor air quality is a big deal.

Mold spores and bioallergens.

Pollutants.

Particulates.

Opportunities

Mold grows on coils, so we're closest to problems.

Energy efficiency more important than ever.

Want speed and innovation.

Not as price-sensitive as OEMs.

Wholesalers.

Want custom designs and smaller batches.

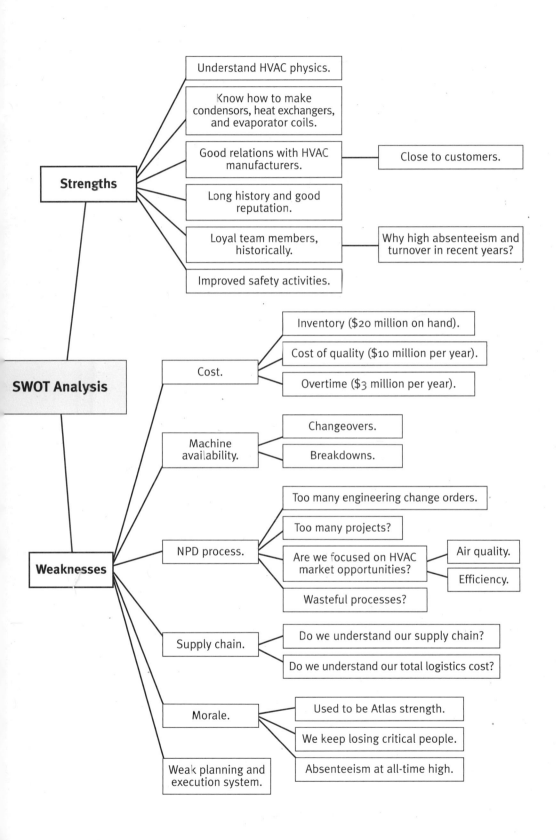

Karras then reminded the team that the strategy deployment process entailed three PDCA cycles: micro (normally weekly to monthly), annual, and macro (every three to five years), and that they would initially focus on the micro and annual cycles.

Sophie Suarez asked why they weren't developing the macro strategy first. Karras explained that the macro cycle was the most difficult. The Atlas team would tackle it once it had grasped the annual and micro cycles. *Speed—Cost—Innovation* would be their guiding light for at least the next year. Then they'd do a reality check and see if it still made sense.

Karras explained that they would be developing "mother" A3 strategies for *Profitability*, *Delivery*, *Customer Satisfaction*, and *Employee Satisfaction* —the second-level focus areas of their planning and execution tree.

Second Level of Tree at Atlas Industries

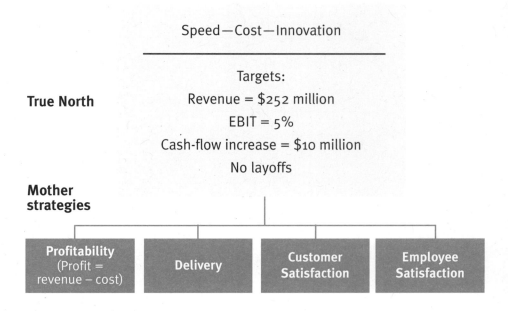

Speed—Cost—Innovation

True North

Targets:
Revenue = $252 million
EBIT = 5%
Cash-flow increase = $10 million
No layoffs

Mother strategies

| Profitability (Profit = revenue − cost) | Delivery | Customer Satisfaction | Employee Satisfaction |

PDCA Cycles

Strategy deployment comprises three Plan-Do-Check-Adjust cycles:

- Micro—normally a weekly to monthly cadence.
- Annual.
- Macro—normally three to five years. (In some changing industries with rapidly changing markets, such as apparel or high-tech, macro cycles will correspond to market conditions.)

The annual and micro PDCA cycles are reactive in the sense that you react to existing quantitative data (e.g., last year's planned and actual results).

The macro cycle is proactive in that you generally have less quantitative data, and must rely more on qualitative data and intuition. Proactive PDCA entails synthesizing into a coherent and compelling image the company's:

- Business need,
- Long-term vision,
- Core capabilities,
- Environmental changes, and
- Values.

That image then informs the annual planning process.

Proactive PDCA is more difficult than reactive PDCA. Understanding this, Karras is teaching the latter to the Atlas Industries team. Once the team has experienced and grasped the annual strategy deployment cycle, they'll be ready to develop a meaningful three-to-five-year strategy.

Cross-Functionality and Deployment Leaders

To encourage cross-functionality, a *deployment leader* was assigned to each focus area. Karras explained the deployment leader role in detail and made the following assignments.

Deployment leader assignments	
Focus area	**Atlas Industries deployment leader**
Employee satisfaction	*Phil Lucas, director HR*
Customer satisfaction	*Bob Jonas, director Quality Assurance*
Delivery	*Carrie Webb, director Production Control & Logistics*
Profitability	*Ed Wolf, director Finance*
Strategy deployment	*Ed Wolf, director Finance*

"Deployment leaders, also known as 'pacemakers,'[2] write the A3 strategy and develop consensus," Karras told the team. "They *wrap their arms around their 'zone'* and tell the story. When a manager signs the A3, she is saying, 'I support this plan and I'll carry out my responsibilities.'

"The A3 is our *hypothesis*. We believe that *these actions*, based on *this* business situation, will achieve *these* results. We adjust our hypothesis based on what we learn."

---

2. Not to be confused with the pacemaker process in a lean value stream, as defined in the *Lean Lexicon* (Cambridge, MA, Lean Enterprise Institute, January 2003).

More on Deployment Leaders

Imagine a rowing team: the coxswain ensures that each member is pulling at the right pace and intensity. Individual efficiency does not equal overall efficiency. Similarly, for planning and execution, deployment leaders ensure cross-functional alignment by:

- ⊙ Leading the planning and execution process.
- ⊙ Writing the strategic planning A3 and developing consensus.
- ⊙ Tracking progress and making "hot spots" visible.
- ⊙ Building required management systems.

Deployment leaders

Deployment leaders are the chief scientists that develop profound knowledge of their "zone," make connections that elude others, and drive action planning. Deployment leaders and operating managers are usually peers, and there needs to be creative tension between the two.

Perhaps the most famous example of a deployment leader is the Toyota "chief engineer" or shusa. The chief engineer for an auto platform like Camry or Corolla has little formal authority and comparatively few direct reports. However, he or she is acknowledged to be the platform's most powerful person to whom even senior executives defer.

Typical deployment leader assignments at Toyota factories

Need	Deployment leader
Safety	*Human Resources*
Quality	*Quality Assurance*
Delivery	*Production Control*
Cost	*Finance*
Culture	*Human Resources*
Environment	*Engineering*
Strategy development	*General Affairs, President's office*

The deployment leader role is essential to breakthrough performance. Many companies that are comfortable with cross-functionality implement the deployment leader concept without difficulty. However, in other companies, the deployment leader may threaten powerful line managers and executives who resist, play games, or simply blow the deployment leaders off, severely hindering improvement.

When implementing strategy deployment, ask questions like:

⊙ Who is the right deployment leader for each objective?

⊙ How do we create understanding of the deployment leader role?

⊙ What obstacles are the deployment leaders likely to face and how do we support them?

⊙ What skills do deployment leaders need and how do we provide them?

Our answers inform our implementation plan.

Focusing the Mother A3 Strategies

"How do we focus our strategies?" Karras asked. The management team was familiar with basic tools such as fishbone diagrams and Pareto charts,[3] but wasn't sure if and how they fit in with strategy deployment. Karras outlined a four-step mental model that showed them the way:

1. *What is the gap?* (What are we trying to improve?)

2. *What's preventing us from meeting our target?*
   (A fishbone diagram shows causes contributing to the gap.)

3. *What are the causes in order of importance?*
   (Pareto chart ranks the causes.)

4. *What actions will address the most important causes?*
   (The A3 sets up the course of action.)

"Most people jump from Step 1 to Step 4," Karras cautioned. "It's human nature. But I want you to hit the 'pause' button. Structure it like an experiment and work backward. 'I believe that these actions will address these causes based on this analysis of this gap.'"

The team absorbed it in silence. By now they knew that clarity and simplicity were hard work. Karras then addressed the deployment leaders. "Your challenge is to get everybody on the same page. Please remember the acid test of any strategy: *Is the story persuasive?*"

---

3. Fishbone diagrams, also known as cause-and-effect diagrams, help to identify the causes of a problem. For more information, see Michael Brassard and Diane Ritter, *The Memory Jogger II, A Pocket Guide to Tools for Continuous Improvement and Effective Planning* (Methuen, MA, Goal/QPC, 1994).

Strategy Development Mental Model

Karras' strategy-development mental model, illustrated below, applies at all levels of the organization. Zoom out to the enterprise level (strategy deployment) or zoom in to solve day-to-day problems.

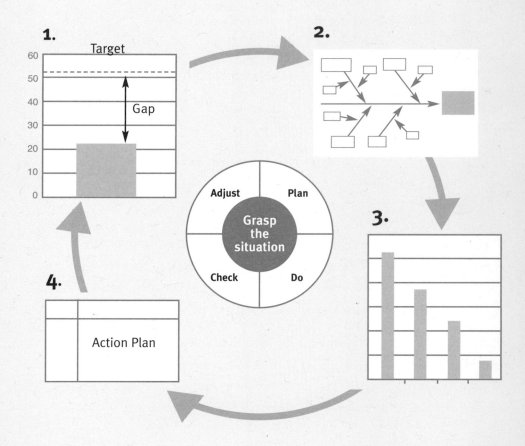

Step 1 defines the gap. It could be an enterprise measure like revenue, or a front-line metric like process time or units per hour. Step 2 asks, "What prevents us?" and encourages brainstorming via a fishbone diagram. For example, in developing his Profitability A3, Ed Wolf will ask, "What prevents us from achieving our financial targets?"

His fishbone diagram might look like this:

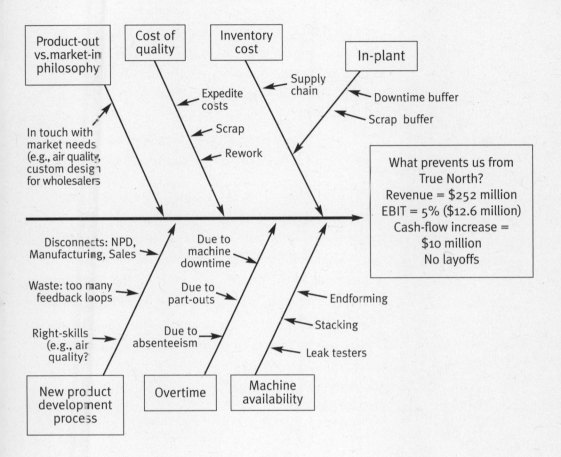

Step 3 prioritizes possible causes in a Pareto chart. Step 4 develops an action plan (hypothesis) and expresses it on an A3.

Here are the most common failures with this approach:

- ⊙ Not defining the gap; initiating activity without understanding what you're trying to improve, or by how much.

- ⊙ Superficial causal analysis.

- ⊙ Not prioritizing causes or prioritizing without data.

- ⊙ Actions don't address the most important causes.

It's All About Emphasis

Over the next few weeks the deployment leaders developed their strategic-planning A3s. They reviewed their value-stream maps, went to the gemba, and talked to their colleagues. Deployment leaders often got sidetracked. Karras kept reorienting them to True North. "We need $252 million in revenue, $12.6 million in EBIT, $10 million in cash flow," he told them, "and no layoffs! If we achieve these results, the rest will follow."

It was hard condensing everything down to one page. Initially, deployment leaders put everything Atlas Industries did into their A3s. They began to understand that it was about *emphasis*. If a given area or activity was in good condition, it need not appear on the A3. Karras encouraged them to think about *deployment* throughout Atlas Industries. They were creating a tree of activities. If there was too much on the mother A3, it would create an unachievable thicket of activities for the supporting A3s at the third and fourth levels.

Here is what Ed did to create and develop support for his A3 strategy.

Ed's *Profitability* A3 was to be the cornerstone of the Atlas strategic plan. To achieve True North, Ed had to address both revenue and cost. Ed realized that he would have to grasp the situation by talking with his colleagues in Manufacturing, New Product Development, and Sales and Marketing—and by going to see the actual condition in each area. The biggest challenge would be getting them to buy into his diagnosis and proposed cure.

He also knew that he'd have to align his activities with those of Carrie and Bob, deployment leaders for *Delivery* and *Customer Satisfaction*; achieving the *Profitability* targets required getting inventory and cost-of-quality waste under control.

Revenue

On the Revenue side, Ed knew that Atlas had to replace the lost Henderson Controls account ($12 million) and prevent further erosion of the customer base. Ed had several informal chats with Jim Torrey, the Sales and Marketing director. He wanted to ensure that Jim had a plan to replace the Henderson Controls account and others that might be at risk.

Jim's team, with Karras' help, was already working on a Sales and Marketing plan. It was a two fold plan that included a defensive approach (detailed assessment of at-risk accounts and preventive steps) and an offensive approach (detailed assessment of the top 10 opportunities and approach plans for each one of the 10 opportunities). Ed also went out on a number of sales calls and sat in on Sales and Marketing planning sessions.

Ed learned that:

- The HVAC market had serious problems with mold and other bioallegens.

- Coil geometry often determined heat transfer efficiency and condensation. Mold grew where there was condensed water.

- Coil coatings were being developed that reduced the likelihood of mold growth.

- New markets were opening up; for example, information technology and medical device HVAC.

Management's Responsibility

Lean thinking is about reducing waste and adding value; employee involvement is the engine of improvement. Lean activities will free up cash currently frozen in inventory or other forms of waste. They'll also free up machine and people capacity.

The benefits of lean thinking fully blossom when management is able to secure new business based on shorter lead times, lower cost, and better quality. This, then, is management's part of the bargain with employees. "You help us find and eliminate waste; we'll give you job security and challenging new business."

⊙ New markets required custom design and quick response, and were normally serviced by wholesalers.

⊙ Wholesalers were less cost-conscious and more innovative than OEMs.

Ed wasn't a marketing person, but he was satisfied with Jim's plan and trusted Jim and his team to deliver—provided they had good products to sell. Jim trusted Ed's grasp of Atlas Industries' financial condition, and he accepted the challenge of shoring up the company's revenues.

Satisfied with the Sales and Marketing plan, Ed focused his revenue-generating activities on New Product Development. Again, he had a series of informal chats with Deb, director of NPD, and Dave Taylor, manufacturing director. He sat in on team meetings and learned there was also a major rift between the functions. Manufacturing considered NPD incapable of designing makeable products; NPD, mostly young engineers, avoided the shopfloor for fear of being yelled at. So they tossed their designs "over the wall" and ran for their lives.

Ed called a meeting with Deb and Dave and told them what he had seen. After some tense moments, they agreed that Ed's assessment was accurate. It took several rewrites of the *Profitability* A3 to get Deb and Dave on the same page. They agreed on concrete steps to improve collaboration between their functions.

Cost

On the cost side, Ed's focus was inventory, scrap, and overtime, where he hoped to secure reductions of $4.5 million, $4 million, and $600,000, respectively. Ed needed $3.5 million more to achieve the EBIT target and was counting on departmental cost-reduction activities to make it up. Certainly, the waste was there. He and Dave had frank discussions about it. Again, Dave was defensive initially, but relaxed when he realized that Ed was looking for solutions, not to place blame.

Ed joined Dave on a number of "waste walks" during which Dave pointed out the main areas of waste. Dave said his plan included quickly making changes through kaizen events focused on:

- Standardized work,

- Downtime and changeover reduction at stacking, bending, and endforming machines, and

- One-piece-flow cells.

Ed didn't really understand manufacturing technology, but he trusted Dave's ability to identify and reduce waste. Dave wasn't an accountant, but he trusted Ed's grasp of Atlas' balance sheet and profit-and-loss statements. After several iterations, they came up with targets for inventory, scrap, and overtime waste reduction, and for process metrics like operational availability.

Ed confirmed these targets and activities with Carrie and Bob, deployment leaders for *Delivery* and *Customer Satisfaction*. He also spoke with Phil, *Employee Satisfaction* deployment leader, about how they might engage team members in waste reduction activities. Phil explained how observation-based safety had engaged team members in safety. He believed that they could extend the process to waste reduction.

Here is Ed's final version of the A3.

(*The right side of an A3 typically also will include responsibilities—persons by name—for each activity. In the interest of space and complexity, these have been omitted*).

Ed told his *story* at the Atlas strategy confirmation meeting. It took him less than 10 minutes; he moved through the A3 paper from top left to bottom right. Here's what he said:

Performance, gaps, and targets:
"My A3 is called *Get Rid of the Waste*. It's not very eloquent, but I'm an accountant after all. That's a joke, everyone. Let's start in the top left corner of the A3. As you can see, we missed our revenue and EBIT targets badly last year. Our condition is clearly in the red. We have tons of waste in our company. I've reviewed last year's profit-and-loss statements, and inventory might be the biggest waste of all. You can see from the chart that last year we averaged 31.2 days on hand—way above our target of 20 days, which hurts cash flow. That's another red. As you'll see, I've also quantified other wastes and my strategy is to find them and get rid of them.

"Our *Profitability* targets for the coming year are revenue of $252 million, EBIT of 5% or $12.6 million, and cash-flow improvements of $10 million. These are stretch goals, no question about it. We've lost Henderson Controls, a $12 million account, and are at risk in other programs, too. With respect to inventory, we have to get it down to 20 days, which will free up $6.3 million in cash. As we've discussed, standard cost accounting is such that reducing inventory initially will negatively affect EBIT. It is what it is. This will sort itself out in subsequent years. By also tracking cash flow we'll have an accurate picture of what's happening. You'll notice, by the way, that I haven't developed three-to-five-year targets for revenue, EBIT, or cash flow. We'll do that next year when we develop our three-to-five-year strategy."

Reflection on last year's activities:

"What did we do last year? What worked and didn't work? As you can see, we wanted to improve our new product development process. I give that activity a red. Our lead times didn't improve at all. We're still getting way too many engineering change orders. I don't have reliable data there, but Deb and I have talked about how we might improve.

"We also wanted to energize our cost-reduction activities and generate sales to wholesalers. We made no real progress in either area. I rate both of these activities red. This is a real problem for us because cost pressure from overseas is intensifying. Here's a big concern: Are we in touch with the market?"

Analysis/Justification to this year's activities:

"As you know, profit equals revenue minus cost—standard cost accounting notwithstanding. That's another joke, folks. We've got problems in both areas. On the revenue side, we're not in touch with our customer. There are real opportunities for custom coil design in computer and medical applications. Wholesalers would love us if we could do it. But we'll have to make smaller batches and deliver them quicker. If we can also get a handle on the mold/air-quality problem, we'll be golden.

"On the cost side, waste is killing us: inventory, cost of quality, operating expenses, material cost, and overtime are hidden bank accounts. If we can cash them out, our EBIT would jump like crazy.

"So next year, we have to:

⊙ Reduce waste in our NPD process and give customers what they want,

⊙ Cash out the hidden bank accounts, and

⊙ Get team members involved in waste reduction. The last one was a not-so-subtle hint from Mr. Karras."

This year's action plan:

"The top box on the right summarizes the *Profitability* action plan. As you can see, some of these activities are high-level. I'm going to depend on each director to translate them into bite-sized action plans. That's what deployment is all about.

"On the revenue side, the goal is to get better products to market quicker. Our process targets are as follows: reduce lead time per launch to six months or less; reduce the number of engineering changes per launch to less than five. I'll let you read the specific activities on your own. Let me emphasize the need to:

- ⊙ Breakdown disconnects between Manufacturing, NPD, and Sales and Marketing,
- ⊙ Learn new technologies, and
- ⊙ Implement standards for throughput, cycle time, and WIP in NPD.

"On the cost side, we need a full-court press on inventory, cost of quality, operating expense, material cost, and overtime. You can see the waste-reduction targets under each category. You'll notice that I'm aiming for $16.4 million—higher than our cash-flow improvement target of $10 million. I figure, why not aim high? I appreciate the directors' support on that one, especially Dave, whose Manufacturing team is shouldering the bulk of the load.

"You also can see that waste reduction will depend heavily on kaizen events. Dave and I agree that it's critical to strengthen the kaizen office. I'll let you read the other activities on your own."

Followup/Unresolved issues:

"These are aggressive objectives, as I said. We're going to need time to do all this stuff. Our biggest time-wasters are too many *meetings* and too much *e-mail*. My finance team is developing guidelines and an action plan for both. It's real simple, as you'll see, but if we stick to it, we'll free up a ton of time.

"Finally, as I said, we have to staff up the kaizen office. Dave is on top of that one. We also have to figure out how to get our team members involved in waste reduction. Phil, Dave, and I are on that one. That's it. Any questions?"

End of January—The Reality Check

Developing and signing off on the Atlas mother A3s had taken longer than expected. "Next year will be much quicker," Karras told them. "We'll have our strategies written and signed off in two weeks or less."

When the strategies were signed off, Karras asked that a large, legible "master schedule" be posted in the Atlas "reflection room." This was a big Gantt chart[4] showing all activities scheduled for the coming year. Karras called a team meeting and told them it was time for a reality check.

"I've got a few questions," Karras said. "Do these activities add up to True North? Are they doable this year, or have we taken on more than we can handle? Should we move some stuff around or even defer it until next year?"

The team consensus was that:

⊙ These activities did indeed add up to True North.

⊙ They were doable this year.

⊙ There were some time conflicts, and some timelines should be shifted.

The first week of February, Atlas Industries had an all-team-member meeting to kick off its strategic plan. Bill Harman opened the meeting by saying, "I've been here all my life, and I've never seen our team so focused and aligned. It's no secret that we've had difficulty the past few years, but now we have a great plan *and* a great team. We're on our way back."

---

4. A Gantt chart is a widely used schedule-monitoring method comprising horizontal bars that show which tasks have to be done and the length of time to get them done. For more information, see: Michael Brassard et al, *The Memory Jogger II* (Methuen, MA, Goal QPC, 1994).

Then he summarized True North, talked about his personal values and beliefs, and introduced the deployment leaders, who presented their A3s. Harman closed the meeting by unfurling a large banner: *Speed—Cost—Innovation*, signing it, and inviting everyone to come up and do the same. Atlas Industries would display the banner and its planning and execution tree in the main entrance to the plant.

The View from Above

"John, I really like these A3 strategies," Harman said. "One page and no bull."

"The team did okay. Not great, but not bad."

"What, you didn't like the strategies?"

"The plans are okay," Karras said. "But deployment is even harder."

"Are we in the game, John?" Harman asked.

"Getting there." Karras told him, "Our thinking is getting clearer; we're starting to speak in terms of data. We're growing some leaders; Ed for one. But we need more, and we'll see whether we get it during deployment."

The View from the Floor

"Nothing's changed on the shop floor, John," Tom Schmidt said. "But I've never seen such intense *talking*. Everybody's been out here, directors and managers, asking questions and poking around. Something's happening, that's for sure."

"How has Dave been?" Karras asked.

"A lot more open," Tom replied. "He got all the team members together, went over our value-stream maps and the company A3 strategies. He answered questions and really seemed sincere. A manufacturing information center is going up this week. Dave calls it a 'reflection room.' He says he wants people to know all the good stuff we're doing."

The Big Questions

What is your organization's strategic plan this year?

How are your organization's strategic plans developed?

How does your organization communicate its strategic plans?

What does your organization's planning cycle look like?

How does your organization avoid silo planning and achieve cross-functionality?

Does your organization conduct reality checks around strategic planning? If so, how?

"What do you want me to do?" asked the manager.

"I want you to reduce waste by $2.7 million this year," said Dave Taylor, Manufacturing director. "I'm looking for it to come from inventory, $1.5 million; cost of quality, $1 million; and overtime, $200,000."

"But how do you want me to do it?"

"Ask yourself, 'What prevents me from doing it?' Look at your value-stream map. Pull in the kaizen group."

"But Dave, we don't have time for this kaizen stuff. We have to make parts. ... "

"A manager's job has two parts," Dave instructed, "and that's routine work and improvement work."

"Can't you just tell me what to do?" said the manager.

"Action without understanding is meaningless," Dave told him. "You need to understand your zone better."

"All right," said the manager, wondering what had happened to "Get'er Done" Dave.

Chapter 6
Do—Deploying Our Plan

As February rolled around, the Atlas team was ready to deploy its mother strategies. We'll focus our attention on Atlas' deployment in its largest function, Manufacturing, and in New Product Development (NPD); deployments also were under way in other functions. Because it is such a large function, Manufacturing requires a tree with functional/departmental A3s to support the mother A3 strategies (*Profitability, Delivery,* etc.). For NPD, a much smaller group within Atlas, an action plan suffices. This chapter illustrates the process through which Dave Taylor, director of Manufacturing, and Deb Kramer, director of NPD, *translate* Atlas Industries' True North and mother A3 strategies into meaningful tactics.

Atlas Strategy to Manufacturing and NPD Strategies

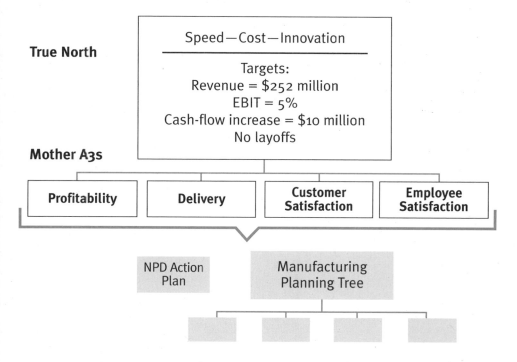

Routine Work and Improvement Work

Managerial work has two parts: routine work and *improvement* work. The formal organizational structure is good at the former, but not so good at the latter because improvement work requires cross-functionality. Moreover, many managers believe their job has no relation to improvement and make no space for it in their daily work. Others would like to make space for improvement work but are overwhelmed by the crises of the day.

Strategy deployment puts improvement work on the radar screen and keeps it there. The planning and execution tree, deployment leaders, and mother A3 strategies provide the cross-functional structure at Atlas Industries that improvement work requires.

Catchball

At the next management team gemba session, Karras introduced the fundamentals of strategy deployment:

1. Move up and down the planning and execution tree.
2. Deploy based on analysis of the current condition at each level.
3. Translate metrics level by level.

He also introduced the *catchball* concept, through which the vision of senior management would be translated into concrete activities throughout the enterprise. Catchball entailed frank, reality-based discussions between and within management levels. The leader normally defined the required result; the team members the means.

Harman and Karras defined True North and tossed the ball to the deployment leaders, who had asked themselves:

⊙ What prevents us from achieving True North?

⊙ Where does *Profitability, Employee Satisfaction, Customer Satisfaction,* or *Delivery* fit in?

⊙ How can we best contribute to Atlas Industries?

Deployment leaders went to the gemba to grasp the situation, talked with their peers and Karras, developed diagnoses, and gained the support for the remedies they proposed. The management team signatures at the bottom of each mother A3, such as the one developed by Ed Wolf for *Profitability,* confirmed alignment.

Catchball

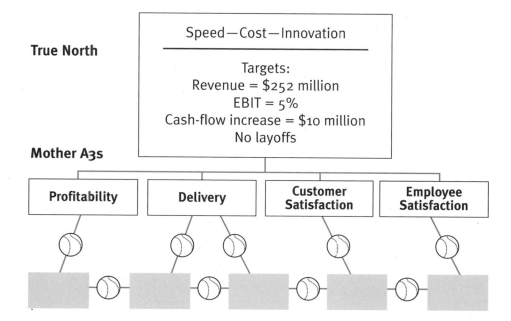

True North

Mother A3s

Speed — Cost — Innovation

Targets:
Revenue = $252 million
EBIT = 5%
Cash-flow increase = $10 million
No layoffs

| Profitability | Delivery | Customer Satisfaction | Employee Satisfaction |

Catchball requires a different kind of leadership and a foundation of mutual respect. The leader trusts the team member's knowledge and ability to achieve the required result. The team member trusts the leader's judgment in picking the right focus area, but is encouraged to push back with facts. Catchball is a scrubbing process that helps management and employees understand what's real.

Creating Baby A3s

Now, Karras explained, the functional directors had to apply the same process—go to the gemba, talk with peers, diagnose problems, gain support, and develop "baby A3s" or actions plans. Directors needed to take into account Atlas Industries' True North and the deployment leaders' mother A3s, and apply the four-step strategy development process:

⊙ What is the gap?

⊙ What's preventing us from meeting our target?

⊙ What are the causes in order of importance?

⊙ What actions will address the most important causes?

Catchball, Karras told them, is a political process in the best sense, but the politics is anchored by data. He reminded the team that "A3s are *shorthand*, a quick, easy way to summarize our thinking, so we can *go do*. So keep it simple. Your baby A3s can be simple action plans or detailed A3s. And some things are 'just-do-its.' You needn't write everything down."

Deployment in Manufacturing—Cost Side of the Equation

Dave and Karras worked together on deployment in Manufacturing. Karras suggested that Dave define True North for Manufacturing and build a tree, as they had done for Atlas Industries as a whole. Dave felt that Manufacturing should focus on waste reduction, and asked Ed how much of the $16.4 million waste-reduction target belonged to Manufacturing. Ed told him about $12 million, and gave him a breakdown.

Dave pulled in his Manufacturing managers, and asked them what they thought about waste reduction as the focus and the $12 million as the target. Dave asked them, "What prevents us from achieving $12 million?" After analysis and more discussion, the Manufacturing team answered that question and defined their department's True North and approach and goals as follows:

True North
Manufacturing
Wring Out the Cost

Targets:
Build to schedule = 90%
Total waste reduction = $12 million
• Inventory = $5.4 million
• Cost of quality= $4.1 million
• Operating expenses = $ 1.8 million+

Wring Out the Cost, they believed, would bring Manufacturing's problems, such as inventory, scrap, and downtime, into sharp focus. It would also support *Speed—Cost—Innovation* and the critical EBIT target of $12.6 million. Ed, the *Profitability* deployment leader, fully supported their thinking.

The Manufacturing team defined the second level of the tree in accord with their organizational structure. Department managers would be deployment leaders.

Manufacturing Department/Function Tree

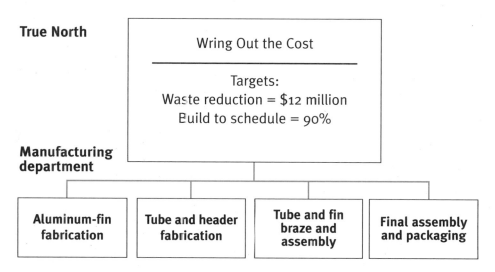

"That should work fine," Karras told them. "But how will you deploy within each department?'

Dave and his team decided that each department within Manufacturing should have a minideployment leader for each mother strategy of *Profitability, Delivery, Customer Satisfaction,* and *Employee Satisfaction.* For example, the aluminum-fin fabrication department would have four deployment leaders. It would be a great way of staying focused and of developing leadership skills in promising group leaders. Deployment leader responsibilities would rotate each year. Over time, they would learn the entire management system.

Karras liked their thinking. "Advanced plants replicate this system to the *team* level. Maybe next year we'll do this. (*See below.*)

"You've made a great start," Karras told the manufacturing team. "Here's a long-term challenge for us. How do we get beyond manufacturing and begin to see the business as our customers see it—an entire product rather than a series of departments?"

They mulled it over. "We'll have to keep an eye on this," said Dave. "I don't have an answer right now."

Karras nodded. "Value-stream thinking—as we get better, we'll introduce more and more of it."

Aluminum-Fin Fabrication Deployment Model—Department Level

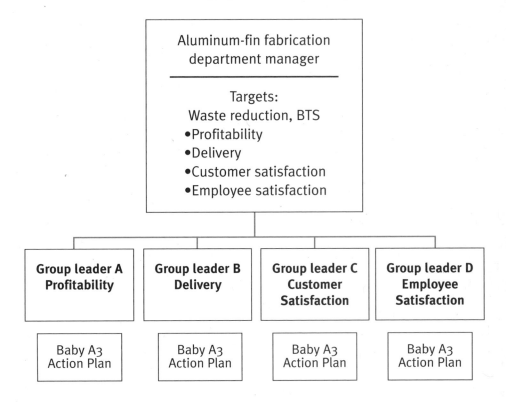

Value-Stream Thinking

The Atlas team is doing a good job of deploying their goals down through their departments. While this traditional structure is comfortable, there are potential drawbacks. Without deployment-leader oversight, departments might optimize measures in their zone without always considering the impact on other areas or on the business as a whole. Such "point optimization" is often seen where kaizens aren't coordinated for a larger purpose.

An approach Atlas could take to resolve this is to identify the total value stream that creates the end product their customers purchase.[6] Once the value stream (the combination of processes rather than process-specific departments) is identified, a value-stream leader could be assigned to ensure departmental efforts are aligned to produce real results for customers.

As noted earlier, in Toyota the chief engineer has this responsibility. He or she is the deployment leader for an auto platform like Camry or Corolla. Although the chief engineer at Toyota has little formal authority, he or she is acknowledged to be to be the platform's most powerful person to whom even senior executives defer.

Eventually, Atlas will need to move to value-stream thinking and may build its organizational structure around value streams rather than traditional functions. Karras has decided to let Atlas get used to the new management methods and deployment process before he introduces value-stream management in a deeper manner. Depending on your situation (e.g., you might have stable operations already), you may want to start with value-stream thinking.

6. For more on value streams, see: Mike Rother and John Shook, *Learning to See* (Cambridge, MA, Lean Enterprise Institute, 1999).

Deployment in the Aluminum-Fin Fabrication Department

Dave deployed the $12 million waste reduction target for Manufacturing to each department. Vic Falcone, manager of aluminum-fin fabrication, accepted the following targets for his department:

Inventory:	$2,000,000
Scrap:	$1,200,000
+ Operating expense:	$700,000
Total:	$ 3,900,000

Vic and his team asked themselves, "What prevents us from achieving $3.9 million in waste reduction?" The team decided that *Delivery*, and more specifically, machine capability, was their biggest obstacle. Stacking, endforming, and leak-testing machines broke down frequently, had long setup times, and often made junk. Vic made his strongest group leader the *Delivery* deployment leader. On the following page is the A3 strategy, *Aluminum-Fin Fabrication Delivery Strategy*.

Vic made a veteran group leader the *Employee Satisfaction* deployment leader, a fellow who had a passion for safety and was well-respected by team members. Uncomfortable with computers, he wrote an action plan in pencil, *Aluminum-Fin Fabrication Employee Satisfaction Strategy—Action Plan*. The group leader set the department's lost-time-case-rate target below that of the plant (1.0 vs. 2.0). "We've done well in safety," he reasoned, "but we should be better next year." Vic agreed.

Manufacturing baby strategies were also developed for *Customer Satisfaction* and *Profitability*.

Deployment in New Product Development — Revenue Side of the Equation

Deb and the NPD team also deployed Atlas' True North and mother A3s. The team's consensus was that NPD could most influence *revenue*. They asked themselves two questions:

⊙ What prevents Atlas Industries from achieving True North?

⊙ How can NPD contribute?

Here's how they answered the first question:

⊙ *NPD had no standards for work-in-process.* This "everything into the hopper" approach overloaded the system and cycle times expanded exponentially. It took forever for new products to get into production.

⊙ *Engineers' utilization rates exceeded 110%.* Engineers' effectiveness decreased sharply above 80% utilization. Turnover was a big problem, and Deb was constantly recruiting and training new hires.

⊙ *The NPD process was wasteful.* There were unnecessary feedback loops, and stage gates were like tollgates—everything stopped.

⊙ *NPD project teams did not sit together.* Sales and Marketing, Manufacturing, and NPD were all represented on project teams, but persons from the different functions rarely saw each other. This was a reflection of the disconnect among the three functions.

⊙ *Product-out mentality.* Atlas' emphasis had always been on getting the product out, not bringing the customer in.

⊙ *The current NPD condition was invisible.* Karras challenged the team to develop a visual tool that would illustrate at a glance all work-in-progress, the current NPD process step for each project, and the top three problems per project.

Jim Torrey, director of Sales and Marketing, also attended and highlighted market opportunities (i.e., how NPD can contribute):

⊙ *Develop coils that reduced or prevented mold buildup.* Jim had heard that polymer coatings were being developed for coils, and the technology held a lot of promise for reducing mold. He also knew that fin structure and geometry largely determined condensation—which caused mold growth.

⊙ *Develop coils with custom fin structures for applications where size and weight were important.* Jim believed that the cooling of medical and computer devices was wide open for new products. Here again, custom fin structure and geometry were key.

⊙ *Work on technologies that not only cooled but cleaned the air as well.*

They answered the second question with an action plan, called *All the Cool Things We Can Do.*

The Deployment Unfolds

In the ensuing months, Atlas directors, managers, group leaders, and team leaders implemented their action plans. Some were good; others not so good. Still it was the best plan Atlas had ever had. Team member commitment reflected Karras' 10-80-10 rule:

⊙ 10% were fully supportive,

⊙ 80% were pleased that Atlas Industries was getting its act together, but they were adopting a wait-and-see attitude, and

⊙ 10% were against it.

Karras called the three groups the *Rowers*, *Watchers*, and *Grumblers*, respectively, and gave his team the following advice:

- *Support the Rowers as much as possible.*

- *Stick to your plan* and over time the *Watchers* will become *Rowers.*

- *Ignore the Grumblers*—they never change.

The Hard Work of 'Do' Begins

Between the deploying and the checking falls the *doing*—the hardest and most important work. Here's what the Manufacturing and NPD functions did as the year progressed.

Manufacturing had a cost focus, and Dave used carefully planned and coordinated kaizen events to get at the necessary gains (staff suggested many other kaizen-event targets, but Dave and his team resisted the temptation for "drive-by" kaizens):

- Standardized work—12 events,

- Changeover reduction—10 events,

- Downtime reduction (maintenance team)—eight events,

- One-piece-flow events—six events,

- Visual management and 5S—four events, and

- Other—three events.

To support the work, Dave expanded his kaizen group and reported their activities in the Manufacturing reflection room. Kaizens were recorded on the value-stream maps for the main product families. The weekly kaizen team report-out was a big deal. Karras was always there and asked challenging questions. Often he brought Harman with him. Word got around that these were meaningful meetings with top brass in attendance, and the employees involved in kaizen teams prepared their presentations carefully.

NPD had a revenue focus. Deb began by taking the cubicles out of the NPD office, which initially upset many. She also persuaded the director of Sales and Marketing (Jim) and Manufacturing (Dave) to collocate appropriate team members in NPD.

Deb established targets for work-in-process (20), projects per engineer (fewer than five), and engineers' utilization rates (80%), and she managed to it. Deb also established an NPD assessment committee comprising representatives from NPD, Manufacturing, and Sales and Marketing. The committee became the gatekeeper for new projects. The NPD team developed a simple financial model that eased the assessment process. The idea was to make good decisions quickly and to control work-in-process.

Deb and her team developed a visual tool modeled on a racetrack. There were 20 lanes, one for each project. You could only add a new project when one had closed or one project was removed. "Close one, start one" became a guiding principle. The racetrack also made report-outs more compelling. These became standup, exception-based events that regularly drew directors, Karras, and Harman.

To reduce NPD's cycle time, Deb asked Dave's kaizen group to pull together a team and conduct a rapid-improvement event. The NPD kaizen team identified unnecessary feedback loops and other waste. They also developed a cell to speed up the engineering change order (ECO) process. Engineers arranged their desks in a U-shaped cell and processed ECOs one at a time. ECOs that had taken days or weeks could now be done in hours.

Strategy deployment created a sense of urgency and direction for using value-stream maps, standardized work, and other lean tools. Skilled leaders used their value-stream maps to identify hot spots. They set standards using the tools of visual management, and engaged team members in developing standardized work.

Atlas' small kaizen group, in place to support events throughout the company, had largely been ignored in recent years except for an occasional Manufacturing event. Now it was starting to get a lot of business and the team was being expanded with new members freed up through kaizen. Because of Atlas' "no layoffs" goal, employees were redirected to help improve and grow the business rather than being let go. In fact, Karras had suggested that when people were freed up through kaizen, the best should be assigned to other areas as this would help spread success quickly.

Manufacturing's renewed use of kaizen events produced a mixed bag of results. Some events were exhilarating and created lasting change; others merely created long punch lists that likely would never get done. Some team members felt their ideas were appreciated and acted upon; others felt that the kaizen team ignored them. All kaizen events were analyzed in order to reap the most improvement, even among events that on the surface looked mediocre—remember, there is a mini-PDCA cycle within the *Do* of PDCA. By spring the Atlas team had palpable momentum.

Kaizen and Involvement

The Atlas team is using its resources well. As noted earlier, the no-layoff goal is a challenge for many organizations but a necessity for transformation. If a company dismisses workers freed up through lean efforts, improvement activity will cease. Also, by staffing the kaizen group with the "best improvers," Atlas provides an added incentive and creates momentum for further improvement.

Karras knows that in the early stages of transformation, optimizing gains is less important than engaging the employees and establishing the discipline of PDCA.

Atlas Movements up and down the Tree

Broad objectives on the Atlas Industries planning tree, such EBIT, have become narrow, process-focused objectives—such as reducing changeover time at a machine or reducing turnover in a given department—deeper down the tree.

Metrics on the Planning Tree

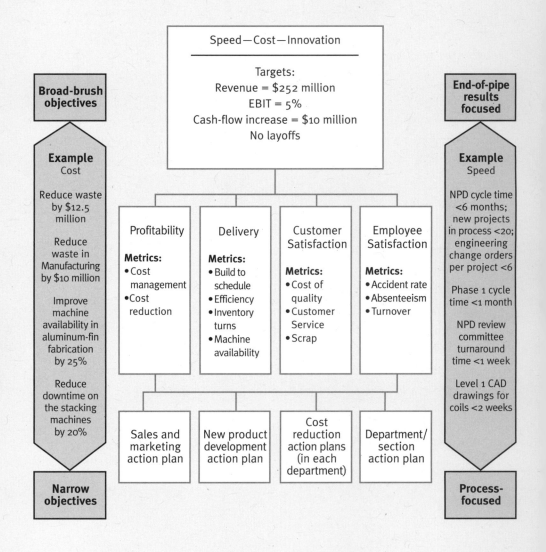

Speed—Cost—Innovation

Targets:
Revenue = $252 million
EBIT = 5%
Cash-flow increase = $10 million
No layoffs

Broad-brush objectives

Example
Cost

Reduce waste by $12.5 million

Reduce waste in Manufacturing by $10 million

Improve machine availability in aluminum-fin fabrication by 25%

Reduce downtime on the stacking machines by 20%

Narrow objectives

End-of-pipe results focused

Example
Speed

NPD cycle time <6 months; new projects in process <20; engineering change orders per project <6

Phase 1 cycle time <1 month

NPD review committee turnaround time <1 week

Level 1 CAD drawings for coils <2 weeks

Process-focused

Profitability

Metrics:
• Cost management
• Cost reduction

Delivery

Metrics:
• Build to schedule
• Efficiency
• Inventory turns
• Machine availability

Customer Satisfaction

Metrics:
• Cost of quality
• Customer Service
• Scrap

Employee Satisfaction

Metrics:
• Accident rate
• Absenteeism
• Turnover

Sales and marketing action plan

New product development action plan

Cost reduction action plans (in each department)

Department/ section action plan

Deployment and the Ladder of Abstraction

Similarly, deployment occurs along a ladder of abstraction for plans (from long-term vision to an annual strategy and down to daily problem-solving) as well as for responsibility among the management hierarchy.

Deployment and the Ladder of Abstraction

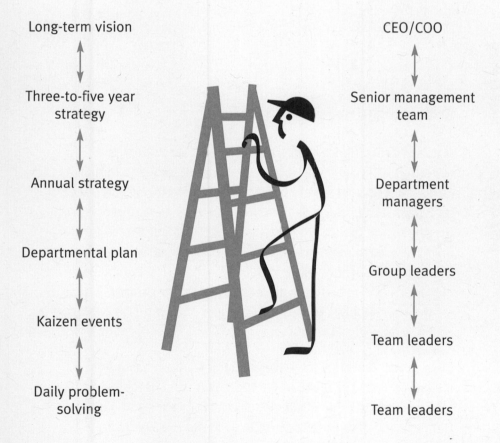

Long-term vision ⇕ Three-to-five year strategy ⇕ Annual strategy ⇕ Departmental plan ⇕ Kaizen events ⇕ Daily problem-solving

CEO/COO ⇕ Senior management team ⇕ Department managers ⇕ Group leaders ⇕ Team leaders ⇕ Team leaders

The View from Above

Karras and Harman were in final assembly and packaging, watching a kaizen event report-out.

"The deployment has gone reasonably well," said Karras. "There's a sense of urgency. We're getting some leadership in Manufacturing and in New Product Development."

"What's next, John?"

"The fun is behind us, " said Karras. "Now comes the hard part—doing all this stuff!"

Invisible Barriers in the System

Company governance systems often create structures and rules that work against strategy deployment and lean thinking. Performance management comes to mind. Managers might hoard resources if their pay level depended on how many direct reports they have and the size of their budgets. The incentive structure might also encourage managers to optimize local efficiency at the expense of overall efficiency. For example, if a purchasing manager's bonus depends on reducing supplier cost, he'll push for the new supplier who is 30% cheaper even if this raises other costs by an order of magnitude.

Such governance issues are beyond the scope of this book. Please be aware of them and of the negative effect they can have on implementation of strategy deployment. (Karras and owner Harman would address them at Atlas in the broader context of organizational change.)

The View from the Shop Floor

Karras and Tom Schmidt were having lunch at a picnic table in the aluminum-fin fabrication department.

"You've put the fear of God into Vic Falcone," said Tom. "Last week Vic had an all-team-member meeting and declared *War on Waste*! Our kaizen team is going again. There's a kaizen status report-out every Monday morning at 10:00 a.m. Not only that, Vic has asked team leaders to start using their boards again. He checks them once a week."

"What do you think is motivating Vic?" asked Karras.

"Vic doesn't want to look bad," said Tom. "Sophie Suarez has some great things going in final assembly."

"Do you think Vic will keep it up?" Karras asked.

"If you check on him, he will," Tom replied.

The Big Questions

How does your organization deploy strategic plans level by level?

How does your organization create alignment around cross-functional goals during strategy deployment?

Evaluate your organization's ability to focus resources.

How does your organization encourage fact-based analysis and discussion around critical strategic goals?

Describe any invisible structures, practices, or rules in your organization that hinder strategy deployment.

"Why is the weekly management meeting so awful?" a director asked.

They'd been at it for three hours and weren't even half way through the agenda.

"It's because we're not prepared."

"Wrong, it's because we have the wrong financial metrics."

"You're both wrong, it's because the right people aren't here."

Karras let it run on like this for another few minutes. Each director had a different opinion.

"What are our hot spots?" Karras asked.

Blank stares.

"What are we doing about them?" Karras continued.

More blank stares.

"From now on, I'd like this meeting to revolve around a simple sequence: Target. Actual. Please explain."

Chapter 7
Check—The Ugly Duckling

It was the end of April and Atlas Industries was beginning to get traction. Jim Torrey's Sales and Marketing plan had already generated promising opportunities. New Product Development hassles were fewer, although Deb Kramer didn't have enough data to prove it yet. Dave Taylor's kaizen events in Manufacturing had generated some gains. Cost-of-quality, build-to-schedule, and cost-per-unit results were all improving. But something was missing.

At the team's next gemba session, Karras reviewed progress to date. Atlas had implemented the first three elements of the strategy deployment system:

1. Define True North—Atlas Industries' strategic and philosophical purpose.
2. Develop the plan (*Plan*).
3. Deploy the plan (*Do*).
4. Monitor the plan (*Check*).
5. Solve problems encountered during implementation (*Adjust*).
6. Improve the system (repeat the PDCA cycle).

Now they had to develop a better *Check* process. The team agreed the weekly management meeting generally was a waste of time. It was a half-day affair held Friday mornings, except when firefighting prevented it.

"It's just a bunch of talk," said Dave. "We rarely follow an agenda; we lack meaningful data. We just go around the table yakking. Everyone feels they have to say something so the discussion develops randomly."

"You know what?" Ed Wolf said. "Team members have a name for it: Atlas talk—in other words, 'Blah, blah, blah.' After some of our meetings I ask myself, 'What the hell was that about?'" ·

"You know what the problem is," Sophie Suarez said. "There is no PDCA in our management meeting."

Checking—The Ugly Duckling

Checking is the ugly duckling of management. We think it's trivial, a job for grunts. Do we reward or recognize good checkers? Yet the PDCA cycle most often stumbles here. Our plan is our *hypothesis*. Checking means comparing *what should have happened* with *what actually happened*—so that we can adjust. No checking, no scientific method.

Checking the quality of another's work is a sign of respect. I remember a visit to a Takaoka plant in Toyota City, Japan. We were following a group leader as he checked standardized work charts in each zone. Each team leader demonstrated a good condition.

"How does this activity benefit the company?" I asked the group leader.

"By checking," he replied, "I show respect for each team leader's activity. I confirm a good condition. And I emphasize our standard."

Exception Management

"Can anyone define the term *exception management?*" asked Karras.

"Exception management means focusing on *hot spots,*" Sophie said.

"Why is it important?" Karras asked.

"Because it will shorten our meetings," she replied. "If we focus on abnormalities, we'll get to problem-solving quicker."

Karras nodded, pleased. "The purpose of plans is to make abnormalities visible so we can fix them. Remember that strategy deployment comprises three PDCA cycles: micro (e.g., weekly to monthly), annual, and macro (e.g., three to five years). This year we'll focus on the micro and annual cycles."

Check Process—Micro PDCA Cycle

Corporate Level

Over the next few weeks the management team transformed its meaningless meeting into a *Check* meeting. Here are the main improvements:

- Rotating focus: The first week was dedicated to *Profitability*, the second week to *Delivery*, and so forth.

- The deployment leader presents the big picture, and function managers present details.

- Dashboards are the main communication tool; each chart has a target line, Red/Yellow/Green assessment, and details in the comment box.

- Exception management: What are the hot spots? What are you doing about them?

- Maximum length: one hour.

It was understood that Manufacturing, the largest function, would usually be the focus.

"How about the *departmental Check* process?" Karras asked.

The Atlas team also agreed that the departmental *Check* meeting should mirror the corporate meeting. Department managers, knowing they were going to be checked on, say, *Profitability*, would in turn check the activities of their group leaders. On the following pages are examples of the corporate and departmental agendas.

Agenda—Atlas Industries Corporate Check and Adjust Meeting
Focus: Customer Satisfaction

1.0 **Current-status summary:** Employee Satisfaction, Delivery, and Profitability
Who: Deployment leaders
Length: About 10 minutes
What: Dashboard, overall comments, announcements, etc.

	Employee Satisfaction summary	Delivery summary	Profitability summary
10 min.	• a ... • b ... • c ...	• a ... • b ... • c ...	• a ... • b ... • c ...

2.0 **Current-status summary:** Customer Satisfaction
Who: Customer Satisfaction deployment leader
Length: About 15 minutes
What: Dashboard showing overall status, "hot spots," countermeasure activities

	Customer Satisfaction aluminum-fin fabrication	Customer Satisfaction tube and header fabrication	Customer Satisfaction tube and fin braze assembly, etc.	Hot spots:
15 min.	• a ... • b ... • c ...	• a ... • b ... • c ...	• a ... • b ... • c ...	Countermeasure activities:

3.0 **Departmental deep-dive report:** Aluminum-fin fabrication (AFF)
Who: Department manager
Length: About 25 minutes
What: Functional dashboards, photographs of activities, etc.

	AFF Customer Satisfaction zone A	AFF Customer Satisfaction zone B	AFF Customer Satisfaction zone C	AFF hot spots:
25 min.	• a ... • b ... • c ...	• a ... • b ... • c ...	• a ... • b ... • c ...	Countermeasure activities:

4.0 **Summary comments:** Big picture, next steps, reinforce values and key objectives
Who: Senior management
Length: 10 minutes

Guidelines:

10 min.	**Alignment:** Reports must link to critical goals set at start of year **Hassles:** Use user-friendly dashboards **Exception management:** Focus on abnormalities

Agenda—Aluminum-Fin Fabrication Check and Adjust Meeting
Focus: Customer Satisfaction

1.0 **Current-status summary:** Employee Satisfaction, Delivery, and Profitability
Who: Deployment leaders (aluminum-fin fabrication)
Length: About 10 minutes
What: Dashboard, overall comments, announcements, etc.

	Employee Satisfaction summary	**Delivery summary**	**Profitability summary**
10 min.	• a ... • b ... • c ...	• a ... • b ... • c ...	• a ... • b ... • c ...

2.0 **Current-status summary:** Customer Satisfaction
Who: Customer Satisfaction deployment leader (aluminum-fin fabrication)
Length: About 15 minutes
What: Dashboard showing overall status, "hot spots," countermeasure activities

	Customer Satisfaction Zone A	**Customer Satisfaction Zone B**	**Customer Satisfaction Zone C**	**Hot spots:**
15 min.	• a ... • b ... • c ...	• a ... • b ... • c ...	• a ... • b ... • c ...	**Countermeasure activities:**

3.0 **Zone deep-dive report:** Weld
Who: Zone group leaders
Length: About 25 minutes
What: Functional dashboards, photographs of activities, etc.

	Weld Customer Satisfaction zone A	**Weld Customer Satisfaction zone B**	**Weld Customer Satisfaction zone C**	**Weld hot spots:**
25 min.	• a ... • b ... • c ...	• a ... • b ... • c ...	• a ... • b ... • c ...	**Countermeasure activities:**

4.0 **Summary comments:** Big picture, next steps, reinforce values and key objectives
Who: Department manager, director
Length: 10 minutes

Guidelines:

10 min. **Alignment:** Reports must link to critical goals set at start of year
Hassles: Use user-friendly dashboards
Exception management: Focus on abnormalities

Team Level

"How about the *team Check* process?" Karras asked.

The consensus was that visual tools were essential for team checking. The manufacturing environment was dynamic, and PDCA had to happen as soon as possible. Strategy deployment had revived team boards at Atlas; they were now in general use, but were focused on routine work, and not improvement work. Dave offered to redesign the boards to get improvement on each team's radar.

Team Boards

A team board is a window on both routine and improvement work. The board on the following page addresses both daily production and strategic issues, and is organized according to SQDCM—*safety, quality, delivery, cost,* and *morale.*

Team objectives and action plans are developed at the beginning of each annual planning cycle. Abnormalities and counter-measures are recorded and tracked manually. Recurrent abnormalities should trigger problem-solving and/or kaizen activity, which should be recorded (e.g., a three-ring binder attached to the board). Teams should review production results daily and strategic results weekly. Corresponding "drills" need to be developed, piloted, and standardized. Please engage team leaders in their development. Routine drives planning and execution.

Zone:

Group Name:

Team

		Concerns	Countermeasures	
S	Date			Who/date
Q	Date			Who/date
D	Date			Who/date
C	Date			Who/date
M	Date			Who/date

Team action plan

Problem-solving

Board

	Tracking	Results

Date									
Day									
Night									
Total									

Date									
Day									
Night									
Total									

Date									
Day									
Night									
Total									

Date									
Day									
Night									
Total									

Date									
Day									
Night									
Total									

activity

Kaizen activity

Production Analysis Boards

Production analysis boards are usually large flip charts or whiteboards. Team leaders record the hourly production plan, actual, and variance from plan. At the end of the shift they summarize the day's results, hot spots, and countermeasure ideas on the team board.

Production analysis boards help to generate "problem consciousness" in team leaders. Hourly checking makes quality, delivery, downtime, and safety hot spots painfully obvious and inevitably dovetails with strategic goals.

"Weekly and daily checking is good," Karras said. "But in Manufacturing and many other functions with shopfloor or office-level activities, we need *hourly* checking and, eventually, unit-by-unit checking. Karras then introduced the production analysis board, which supported hourly checking by team leaders. "The more frequently we check," he said, "the less there is to correct."

Karras also presented a sample chart from his previous company, *Paint Shop Analysis Board*.

Karras explained that the plant from which the production analysis board was taken was in launch mode, and the results reflected it. That was the point—problems were visible. Each hot spot generated intense problem-solving on at least an hourly basis. Production analysis boards were the key to zone control.

The management team was impressed. "This would be a major step forward for us," said Dave.

"Dave, please develop a supporting drill with your team," Karras said. "Involve your team leaders and Phil Lucas and his HR team. We need a standard way of starting and ending each shift, based on the PDCA cycle. I want each shift to be run like an experiment. *Here are our objectives today; here's what actually happened. Here's what we learned, and what we're doing about it tomorrow.* You know what to do: engage, pilot, confirm, and roll out fully—then check it again."

And they did.

Example of a Production Analysis Board

Paint Shop Analysis Board

Date:		Shift:				Superintendent:			
		Zone A		**Zone B**		**Zone C**		**Zone D**	
Hour	Production plan (hr/cumulative)	Actual production (hr/total)	Offline repairs	Actual production (hr/total)	Offline repairs	Actual production (hr/total)	Offline repairs	Actual production (hr/total)	Offline repairs
1	60/60	50/50	5	55/60	3	50/60	9	48/48	11
2	60/120	55/105	7	50/105	7	53/103	6	52/100	7
3	60/180	49/154	8	55/160	3	57/160	1	53/153	6
4	60/240	50/204	7	58/218	1	55/215	4	56/209	4
5	60/300	44/248	13	57/275	2	51/266	8	50/259	9
6	60/360	50/298	3	50/325	8	51/317	7	47/306	12
7	60/420	39/337	18	55/380	4	56/373	3	50/356	8
8	60/480	53/390	5	56/436	2	50/423	9	45/401	13
9									
10									
Total	480	390	66	436	30	423	47	401	70
Top three problems		Metal quality — dents, dings, creases, weld spatter		Primer coverage thin in trunk area		Enamel coverage thin or rocker Overspray—wheel wells		Dirt and spits on roof Mars—left fender	
First-time through[1]		(480 – 66 – 30 – 47 – 70)/480				58%			

1. First-time through (FTT) is a measure of process capability:
   FTT = [Production target – all backflows (e.g. scrap, rework)] ÷ Production target

Check Process—Annual PDCA Cycle

"So what should the annual PDCA cycle look like?" Karras asked at their next gemba session.

"It should mirror the finance cycle," said Ed Wolf. "We have an annual financial plan, and periodic checks to make sure we're on track. We also have midyear and yearend reviews."

Karras nodded. "Our annual PDCA cycle has three milestones: Strategy development and kick-off, midyear review, and yearend review." Karras and the team developed a corresponding timeline.

Check Phase—Annual PDCA Cycle

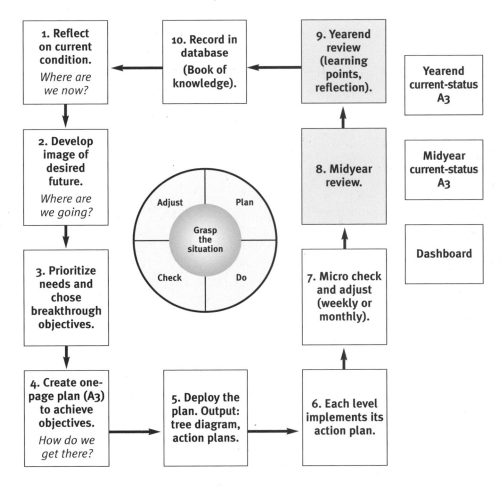

Focus:

Month	Activity
November 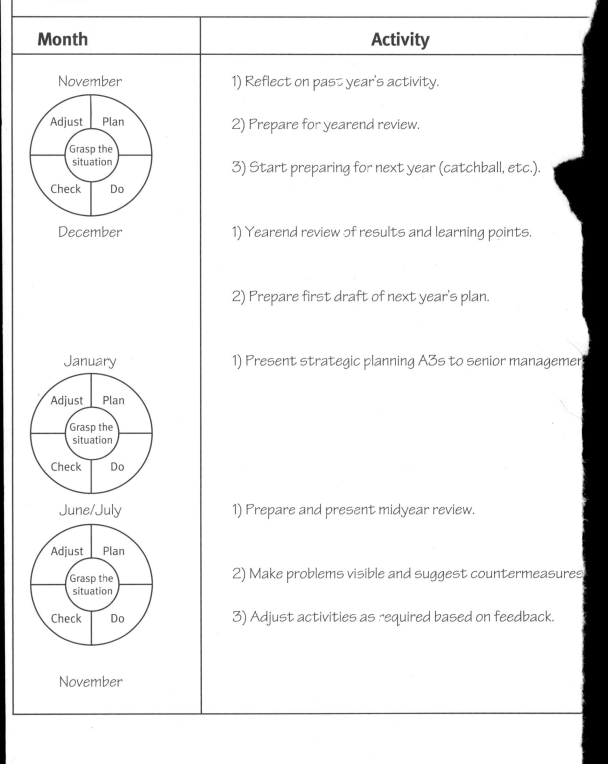	1) Reflect on past year's activity. 2) Prepare for yearend review. 3) Start preparing for next year (catchball, etc.).
December	1) Yearend review of results and learning points. 2) Prepare first draft of next year's plan.
January	1) Present strategic planning A3s to senior managemen[t]
June/July	1) Prepare and present midyear review. 2) Make problems visible and suggest countermeasures 3) Adjust activities as required based on feedback.
November	

Dept:	
	Comment
	Budgets should be developed after our plans.
	Use current-status A3.
	Senior management feedback and reflection.
	Yearend review A3 goes into "Book of Knowledge."
	Confirm alignment through catchball.
it.	Develop feedback protocal: Who speaks and in what order?
	Assign someone to record commitments made.
	Senior management provides guidance and support.
	Direction should already be confirmed through catchball.
	Use current-status A3.
.	Senior management provides guidance and support.
	Weekly check will keep current status visible.
	Formal review—June and December—should hold no surprises.
	Cycle repeats.

Midyear and Yearend Reviews

"Why bother with formal reviews at midyear and yearend?" Karras asked. "Isn't the weekly check adequate?"

"Midyear and yearend reviews are big-picture checks," said Dave. "We'll have been at our strategies for several months. It makes sense to see how things are going."

Karras nodded. "Formal reviews give us a chance to reflect. Have our hypotheses worked out? Why or why not? What adjustments do we need to make? We use the current-status A3 for midyear and yearend reviews." He passed one out: *Midyear and Yearend Review Template*.

Karras pointed out that for each focus area, *three* pieces of paper would enter the Atlas database or "Book of Knowledge" at yearend: strategic planning A3, midyear A3, and yearend current-status A3s ("yearend review").

Current Status A3

The current-status A3 is used at midyear and yearend reviews. Deployment leaders summarize the current condition in their area of focus, including end-of-pipe targets (bottom-line/downstream) and process targets (upstream). The template encourages "*Target. Actual. Please explain.*"

Midyear and Yearend Review Template

Focus/Goal:			Current-Status A3 /

Overview			Target

Goal	Targets	Activities	YTD Results	
			Target	Actual

Yearend Review

Deployment leader

	Actual	Rating	Comments

Rating	Comments / Concerns	Next steps / Learning points

Creative Tension

At the next gemba session, Karras told the team, "We need *creative tension* between deployment leaders and operations. Deployment leaders grasp the big picture and make connections others don't. For example, Bob Jonas, our *Customer Satisfaction* deployment leader, can see the connection between activities in aluminum-fin fabrication and defects in final assembly. He sees the effect of disconnects between New Product Development

The Book of Knowledge—Our Database

The philosopher George Santayana was right: "Those who forget the past are doomed to repeat it." But to remember the past (i.e., to do a "Santayana review"), we need a database.

Some activities entail high-frequency cycles that generate plenty of data. A utility, for example, issues thousands of invoices every month. By tracking errors and analyzing causes, they can make big improvements.

Other activities, like strategic planning, new product development, and market research consist of low-frequency cycles and generate much less data. Santayana reviews support learning. Each annual PDCA cycle ends with reflection and learning points. We need to make them accessible.

The Book of Knowledge should be part of a learning management system. Describing its components is beyond our scope. Some companies develop effective online systems, which offer key word searches and other functionality. Other companies use a simple binder system with dividers for each focus area (e.g. Profitability, Delivery, etc.). Both methods work. The point is, do it.

and Manufacturing. Deployment leaders must challenge the team—'*Look here, here, and here! We're not as good as we think we are!*' Deployment leaders must be strong and hold to the vision expressed in our mother A3s. If operations folks come to me and complain about you, I'll know you're doing your job!"

Atmosphere

A few weeks later Ed, Dave, Sophie, and Karras were having dinner at the Imperial Bar & Grill. They'd had their weekly Atlas *Check* meeting that day, and it was tough one—all sorts of problems, but little evidence of problem-solving.

"John, I'm really struggling with something," Dave said.

"Out with it," Karras replied.

"We heard a lot of problems today, but few solutions. Why didn't you get upset with anyone?"

Karras took a sip of wine. "When mistakes occur, I try not to blame people. Some may think I'm too gentle. Let me tell you a story. Once, when I was a young engineer, I make a big mistake. Had my boss found out, I would have been barbequed. So I kept quiet and asked my buddies to do the same. I covered up my mistake. If I hadn't been afraid, I'd have fixed the problem properly. So I promised myself, when I became a leader, I wouldn't blame my team members.

"Checking requires an atmosphere conducive to reporting mistakes. If someone gets barbequed, is he

Connected Checking

Effective *Check* cascades up and down. Knowing they're going to be checked, each level prepares in advance. For example, knowing that he's going to report out at the corporate *Check* meeting on Thursday, Vic Falcone, manager of the aluminum-fin fabrication area, will check his group leaders on Tuesday. Knowing this, Vic's group leaders will check their team leaders on Monday.

Checking helps to make the important urgent. In the absence of sustained checking, the day-to-day inevitably *crowds out* strategic initiatives.

Connected Checking

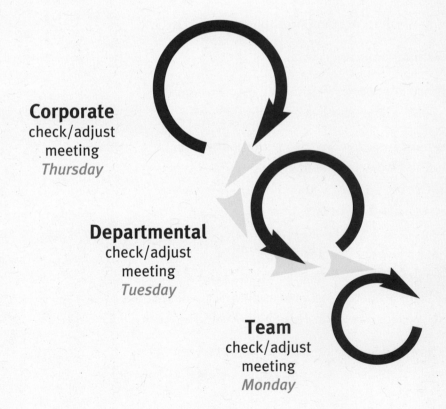

Corporate
check/adjust
meeting
Thursday

Departmental
check/adjust
meeting
Tuesday

Team
check/adjust
meeting
Monday

likely to be honest the next time? If the leader yells and screams, will team members approach her?

"I'm very demanding." Karras said. "I *insist* on countermeasures. But mistakes are bound to happen. If they aren't reported freely, we can't make progress."

The View from Above

Harman and Karras were returning from a supplier visit. Harman was pleased with the Atlas team's progress. "Our numbers keep getting better, John!"

"The silos are beginning to break down," said Karras, "and we're getting pockets of PDCA. Machine availability and scrap are improving, especially in aluminum-fin fabrication and final assembly and packaging. Inventory and expediting costs are coming down nicely, too; there's less instability to buffer."

"Sounds like progress to me," said Harman.

"Yeah, but we're inconsistent," Karras replied. "Even the so-called good departments are all over the place week to week."

"What do we do?"

"Grow more problem-solvers," Karras replied.

The View from the Floor

The aluminum-fin fabrication kaizen report-out had gone reasonably well. Afterward, Karras went for a walk with Tom Schmidt.

"We're definitely moving, John," Tom said. "Changeover times over in stacking are finally coming down. The kaizen team videotaped the process and trained all the operators. We found a lot of waste."

"What do team leaders think of the production analysis boards?" Karras asked.

"The good ones are doing it," Tom replied. "Vic is turning up the heat."

"Anything I can do?" Karras asked.

"We need a simple way of solving problems," Tom said. "Some of us know what to do when we find them, but we don't attack them in a systematic way."

The Big Questions

Describe your organization's corporate, departmental, and team-level *Check* processes.

How does your organization reflect on lessons learned during the strategic planning process?

How does your organization apply the lessons learned?

How does your organization make problems visible?

What is the atmosphere around checking in your organization?

It was the end of the shift, and the group leader was reviewing the zone B production analysis board. Dave Taylor, the Manufacturing director, walked over and asked how the shift had gone. The group leader told him that things had gone pretty well and reviewed the board with Dave.

"Our first time through was 82%, which is good for us. We made 984 units out of 1,200, and we had to run some overtime to catch up."

"What were your biggest problems?" Dave asked.

"We lost 84 units because our clinch line was down; 61 because the braze oven that feeds us is acting up. I lost another 37 because they changed the schedule on me, and I couldn't get the right coils."

"What are we doing about the clinch line?" Dave asked. He knew that there were kaizen events planned to tackle braze-oven availability and scheduling hassles.

"I pulled in maintenance, and last weekend they steam-cleaned the entire line. They found broken sensors and wires and all sorts of oil leaks. We need better downtime data, so we put together a check sheet for the operator. My gut tells me it's the lube system. Oil leaks mean downtime."

"Any way we can reduce cycle time?" Dave asked. "The clinch line's a bottleneck."

"Don't I know it!" said the group leader. "I've got an engineer working with me on that one. We figure we can easily shave 10 seconds or so at the inspection station with light screens, and another 10 seconds at the clinch station just by reprogramming the PLC-6 processors. The robot arm is moving way more than it needs to."

"Good work," Dave said, "and please continue."

Chapter 8
Adjust—The Great Detective

Problems are nuggets to be mined, Karras had said, not garbage to be buried. Nobody argued. Almost everyone in the company had had some training in problem-solving techniques, but they hadn't been widely accepted on the shopfloor and problem-solving skills remained uneven. Some people didn't grasp that they were still in the strategy deployment process. Problem-solving was the logical outcome of the *Check* process.

Many people struggled with Karras' simplest questions:

- ⊙ What is the *point of cause*, the time and place at which the abnormality is occurring?

- ⊙ What is the root cause?

- ⊙ Have you tested for cause and effect?

- ⊙ What are your temporary and permanent countermeasures?

- ⊙ How will you confirm them?

The Atlas Industries management team recognized they had a problem. At a weekly *Check* meeting in September, Dave Taylor asked Karras for more help and insights with problem-solving. Through the training-room window they could see rotary brazing tables, hot torches, and fumes being sucked into exhaust hoods. Later they would head out there to review a kaizen focused on the rotary table.

Adjust

We underestimate the *Adjust* phase of the scientific method (PDCA). We see it as a minor tweak, a slight shift in position. In fact, *Adjust* is detective work, piecing through fragments of evidence as we seek the immediate and root causes of abnormalities. *Adjust* challenges us, as a mystery challenges a great detective. Our nemesis is entropy, the tendency of all things to fall apart—Murphy, if you will.

It's an endless game. Thus we seek *countermeasures*, understanding that problem-solving is endless, and permanent solutions unlikely. Adjust also means standardize if everything goes according to plan, but that's rare. Murphy rules the universe, so we're wise to develop *problem-solvers*—the more the better.

The Adjust Phase

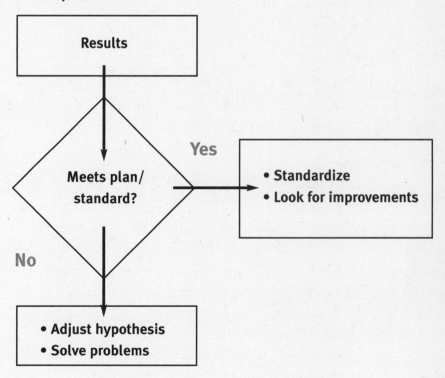

Getting the Right Things Done

"You've learned problem-solving techniques," said Karras. "That's good. We need them to solve complex process problems; for example, leaks related to braze chemistry. But what are our most common problems?"

"Basic stuff," Sophie Suarez said, "like wrong and missing parts, and fin damage. Things that everyone is aware of every day."

"So what kind problem-solving approach do we need?" continued Karras.

"We need to create problem-solvers at Atlas Industries," said Karras. "We need to leverage the knowledge, experience, and creativity of *all* our people. I want *everyone* to solve problems. Your job as leaders is to teach them how and to create a supportive atmosphere.

Science Degree for a Good Scientist?

People who lack technical credentials are often intimidated by problem-solving. They feel that they are somehow incapable or unworthy. Not true! You don't need to have a science degree to be a good scientist. Problem-solving is organized common sense.

Problem-Solving = Organized Common Sense

What does it take to be a good scientist?

- Sound, standardized approach

- Objectivity
  - It is what it is.

- Curiosity
  - Why do things work the way they do?

- Creativity
  - How do I adjust my hypothesis?

"We have a handful of big problems and some medium-sized problems, which we're addressing through our strategic planning process. But we also have to hit all the smaller day-to-day problems that often add up to big problems. That's why we need problem-solvers at all levels." Karras drew it out on the whiteboard.

Problem-Solving Opportunities at Atlas Industries

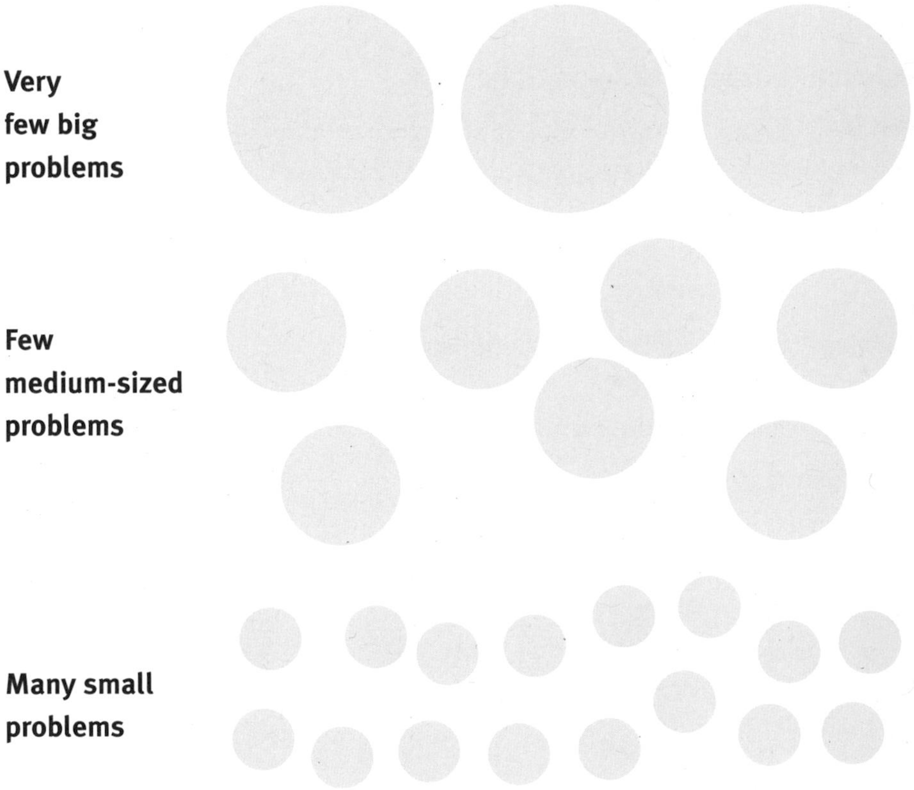

**Very
few big
problems**

**Few
medium-sized
problems**

**Many small
problems**

Here's the interesting thing: it's the same way of thinking at every level. People trained in advanced statistical techniques will find it simplistic, but most problems we run into on a daily basis require basic analytical skills. In fact, calling it problem-solving might be a misnomer. It's a critical and logical thinking process that informs all of strategy deployment. With practice the process becomes second nature and we can use it wherever we need improvement. Sometimes the process occurs over days, months, or even years. Other times it happens in a matter of minutes.

Problem-Solving Activity at Atlas Industries—Long-Term Image

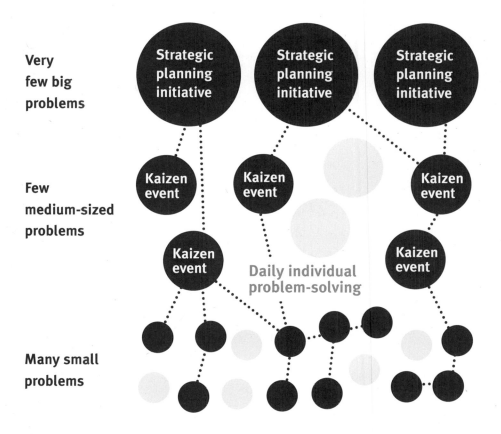

The Improvement Process

"The same thinking that guides our strategy deployment guides problem-solving," said Karras. "It's the same pattern on a smaller and smaller scale. We start with a problem—that is a deviation from a standard or target. We do a causal analysis, using tools such as fishbone diagrams. Then we prioritize what we've found in a Pareto chart. Finally, we make our action plan based upon the Pareto—each action should correspond to an item from the Pareto chart, in descending order of importance."

"Here are some of the situations in which I've seen the process used:

- Team-member skill development,
- Cost reduction,
- Machine availability and performance,
- Kaizen events,
- Productivity and process improvements, and
- Strategic planning and execution.

"In any event, let's take it from the top. *What is a problem?*"

"A problem is a pain in the butt!" Vic Falcone sang out. "It's what keeps you up at night," said Bob Green. "Something weird, something out of standard," said Jose Cano. Manufacturing managers knew all about problems.

Standards

Our standards are not those of traditional engineering: complex, remote, and unchanging. Our standards are simple, point-of-use, and changeable tools—pictures of "what should be happening." We understand there is no one best way. Standards will change as we figure out better ways to do the work. Moreover, we'd like to engage our team members and team leaders in developing standards—they know the work best. Engineers and other specialists will support them as required.

In strategy deployment, the *Plan* is the standard. Thus, a deviation from an expected result in the action plan is a problem to be solved.

Standards and Five Levels of Capability

Level 0: No Standards. Every day is a new day. Roll the dice and hope for the best.

Level 1: Standards exist, but they are not followed. The standards might be in a binder on an engineer's bookshelf, in a complex product specification, or even posted lineside, but they just aren't followed.

Level 2: Standards exist, and they are often followed. Team members have been engaged in standards development, but follow-through is not always consistent.

Level 3: Standards exist, and they are followed. When there is an abnormality, everyone follows a shared and **standardized problem-solving approach**.

Level 4: Evolutionary learning and a broad mastery of tools, techniques, and philosophy acquired through years of practice and reflection. Such mastery fosters the creative state some have called **"unconscious competence."** I've seen it in great athletes and in the master group leaders at Toyota's great "mother" factories: Takaoka, Tsutsumi, and Motomachi.

Problem Consciousness

What should be happening? (Standard) ························

Gap = Problem

What is actually happening?

Karras liked the last answer. "A problem is an abnormality, a deviation from a standard. If we can define 'what should be happening' and 'what's actually happening'—then we have *problem consciousness*. We're in the game. If not, we're lost." He drew it out on the whiteboard and pressed the "print" button.

"So why are we having so much difficulty solving problems?" Karras went on.

"Because we don't know what's happening," Dave said, "or what should be happening."

Karras nodded. "To make problems visible, we need standards for each of the four Ms: man/woman, method, machine, and materials.

"And," Karras added, "depending upon the size of the problem, we tailor the problem-solving approach and the tools at our disposal. There's a number of approaches I want to share with you."

Problem-Solving Approaches

Karras wrote out the following list of approaches that he had found useful at other companies:

- ⊙ Seven-step problem-solving process for medium-sized problems,

- ⊙ Problem-solving funnel to differentiate vague concerns from problems to be solved,

- ⊙ Five-Why analysis to drill down to the root cause,

- ⊙ Four-step problem-solving process, which is applied to daily small problems, and

- ⊙ One-page problem-solving template that incorporates the four-step process.

Karras diagrammed the seven-step approach. It is also known as the "W-V model" because of its shape. He explained that this worked well for the medium-size problems that Atlas addressed through kaizen events and quality circles.

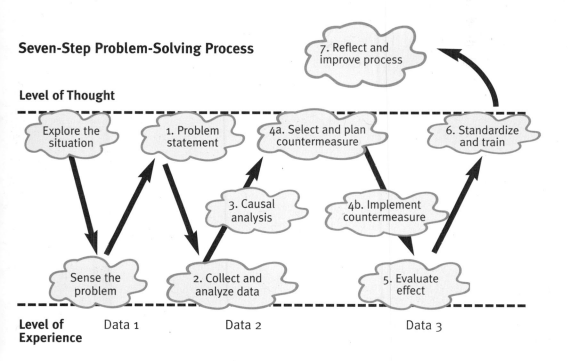

Seven-Step Problem-Solving Process

Level of Thought

7. Reflect and improve process

Explore the situation

1. Problem statement

4a. Select and plan countermeasure

6. Standardize and train

3. Causal analysis

4b. Implement countermeasure

Sense the problem

2. Collect and analyze data

5. Evaluate effect

Level of Experience   Data 1   Data 2   Data 3

Karras reminded the group of the continual movement between the levels of thought and experience. "To formulate our problem statement correctly," Karras said, "we have to find the right level on the ladder of abstraction. For example, is our problem statement: 'The machine is breaking down?' Or is it: 'Our daily production total was 900, and our target was 1,200?'"

"The latter statement is more compelling," said Sophie. "We have a target and an actual for critical goal—production."

"We need to define our problem in a compelling way," Karras agreed. "Problem-solving, like strategic planning, is *storytelling*. We don't want people to think 'who cares?' when they hear our problem statement!" He then drew a diagram of a *problem-solving funnel*.

Problem-Solving Funnel

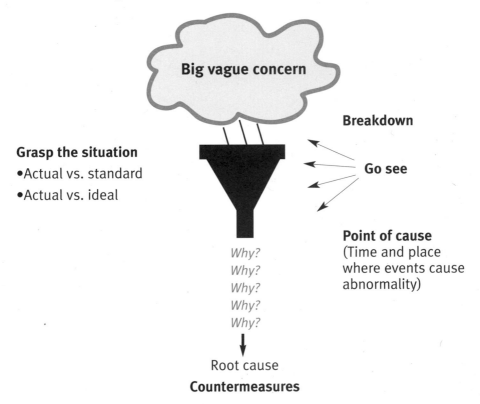

"This can help differentiate between a *concern*—simply a vague sense that there was something wrong—and a *problem* or deviation from a standard."

The funnel model was clear to the management team, the members of which were familiar with Five-Why analysis. Karras pointed out that Five-Why analysis was another example of the ladder of abstraction.

Five-Why Analysis and the Ladder of Abstraction

Problem statement:
We only made 900 units.
Why?
The robot stopped.
Why?
It was overloaded and a fuse blew.
Why?
The arm wasn't adequately lubricated.
Why?
The lubrication pump wasn't working.
Why?
A part of the pump was worn out.
Why?
Dirt and debris entered the pump shaft.
Why?
The pump motor was designed without a filter.

Five-Why analysis entails moving up and down the ladder of abstraction. To formulate a compelling problem statement, find the right level of abstraction, as noted in the text. Then ask "Why" continually until the root cause of the problem is found. You can have fewer or more levels based on the situation.

"As I said, the seven-step problem solving works well for kaizen events and quality circles," Karras went on. "For day-to-day problem-solving, we can condense it to four steps. We want something simple and robust that everyone can use."

Karras drew a four-step problem-solving process, which Atlas Industries would use for daily problem-solving.

To illustrate, Karras asked the management team to form small groups, and he then gave each group a case study. The model had seemed simple, until they tried to apply it to their case study. Then Karras asked each group to select an actual problem to attack. He also passed out a problem-solving template that incorporated the four-step process, and told each team to explain their problem-solving at the next session.

At their next gemba session, Sophie's report-out was first. She passed out her team's problem-solving one-pager, *Problem Investigation—Ergonomics*.

Four-Step Problem-Solving Process

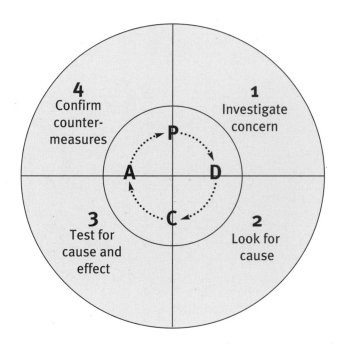

Problem Investigation—Ergonomics

Description:	Current standard:	Date: Sept. 29
Hose hard to attach to coil • Ergonomic force = 12 kg-f (sore hands). Three lost-time injuries in the past year • Cycle time hard to meet (15+ sec) • Quality concern (~10 split hoses per day)	• <7 kg-f (ergonomic standard—new) • 8 sec (element cycle time) • No split hoses	**Department/Zone/Shift** Final assembly Zone B Shift 1 Process 7 **First observed (date/time):** July 15

Problem investigated by: Sophie Suarez and team   **Repeat item:** (Yes) No

Causes: [Use fishbone on back if necessary]
Coil coupling too big for hose. Outer diameter standard = 2 cm; Actual = 2.2 cm

Root Causes: [Use Five Whys]
1. No quality confirmation at process 7, line 4 in tube and header; easy to pick wrong coupling; no visual control or emphasis.
2. Incoming quality of couplings not checked in final assembly.
3. No ergonomic standard.

Cause and effect confirmed: (Yes) No   **How:** Tried it myself.

Countermeasures:

	What	Who	When
Temporary/ Immediate	• Provide lubricant to reduce force needed • Order heat lamps	• Team leader	• Immediately
Permanent	• Communicate standard to tube and header fab	• Group leader	• Immediately
	• Visual control, error proofing at process 7, line 4	• T&H fab	• ASAP
	• Screen/report coupling status	• Team leader	• Tomorrow
	• Identify similar problems	• Group leader	• Group leader

Review standardized work:

(Exists) Does not exist   (Followed) Not followed   Adequate (Not adequate)

Followup Action: Track on team board   Weekly followup with T & H fab

[Confirm countermeasures]

	What	Who	When
	• Confirm process 4, line 7 improvements	• Group leader	• End of week
	• Review coupling quality report	• Team leader	• End of week
	• Confirm lubricant and heat lamps	• Team leader	• End of week

"We went after an ergonomic problem in final assembly in keeping with our *Employee Satisfaction* action plan. We've had three lost-time injuries there in the past year. Team members can't complete the process within cycle time; team leaders have to help. We also get an average of 10 split hoses per shift, which we have to repair offline."

"To get to root cause, we did a fishbone and Five-Why analysis," Sophie noted. "It's a safety, quality, and throughput problem—and we just lived with it."

"Any learning points?" Dave asked.

"You've got to have a standard," a team member said. "Go see what's actually happening," said another. "Keep asking 'Why?' until you get to root cause," said yet another.

"Do you think you can learn to apply the four-step process?" Dave continued.

"I think so," said the team member. "Without a process, we would've been lost."

Support for Problem-Solving

That night John, Dave, Sophie, and Ed had dinner together at the Imperial Bar & Grill. "Problem-solving won't stick unless you develop a support plan," Karras told them.

"We're way ahead of you, John," said Dave. He showed Karras the mind map they'd been working on, which would become their support plan. They planned to implement it over the next year.

"Sophie and I are going to drive it," he said.

Atlas Industries' Problem-Solving Support Plan

Objectives: To improve problem-solving capability at all levels.
Targets: All team leaders and above trained in four-step process by March 30.
Problem-solving process used widely and visibly by June 30, next year.

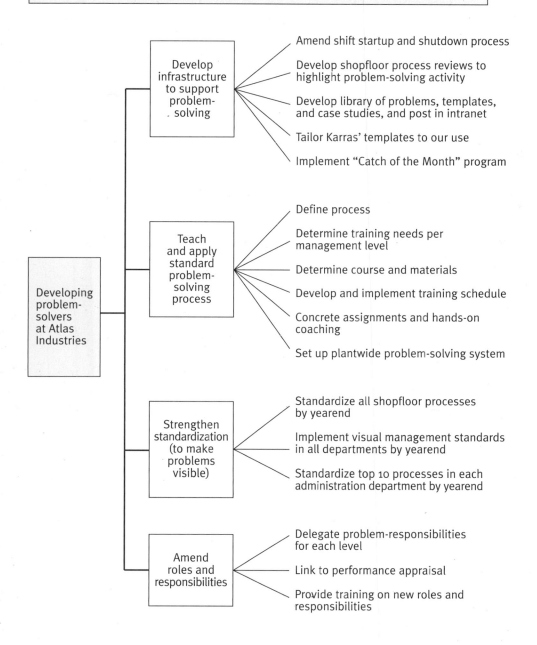

The View from Above

Karras and Harman were driving back from a customer presentation. Deb Kramer's NPD team had designed a coil whose size, geometry, and performance made it ideal for cooling computer equipment and, possibly, medical equipment. The customer, one of the largest wholesalers in the industry, was extremely interested. Jim Torrey, director of Sales and Marketing, had said, "Finally, something cool to sell." Dave had confirmed that Atlas could produce it profitably in the small batches the customer required.

Harman was delighted. "We're on a roll, John!"

"This could be a big break for us," Karras agreed. "We got that prototype built in record speed. Deb, Jim, and Dave worked well together."

"Are we in the game, John?"

"Yes, we are, Bill. We're improving across the board: downtime, scrap, inventory, and efficiency. Problem-solving isn't a habit yet, but we're getting some great leadership from Dave."

"What's next, my boy?"

"We've got pockets of stability," Karras replied. "Now we have to tie it all together. Remember our recipe?"

"*Stabilize, flow, pull*, and *seek perfection*," Harman replied.

"Bill, as my dad would say, you're a *phenomenon*."

The View from the Floor

Karras and Tom Schmidt had just attended the daily shipping-quality audit at the final line. The table was covered with the past week's casualties, and the responsible group leaders had presented their countermeasure activities.

"We're getting some intense problem-solving, John," Tom said. "The group leaders prepare for this report-out like crazy."

"Why all the intensity, Tom?" Karras asked.

"Because they know you'll be there," Tom replied, "and Dave and all the managers, too. It's a big deal."

"How is the four-step problem-solving process going over?" Karras asked.

"We like it," Tom said. "It's understandable and it works."

The Big Questions

What happens in your organization when a plan or standard is not met?

Describe your organization's cultural mindset around problem-solving.

How does your organization support and encourage problem-solving?

What happens in your organization when people report problems?

Evaluate the problem-solving capability in your organization.

What steps would you take to improve problem-solving in your organization?

It was Atlas Industries' yearend report-out. Carrie Webb, the Delivery deployment leader, had given the inventory result a red rating even though Atlas had reduced the number of inventory days by 15% and had saved $2.6 million.

"How can this be a red, Carrie?" Bill Harman asked. "I believe this is the best inventory result we've ever had."

"I'll answer that," said Dave Taylor. "Our target for inventory days was 20, and our actual was 26.4 days. We're way off; that's a red."

"Why were you way off target, Dave?" Harman asked.

"In retrospect, I think our target was unrealistic," Dave replied. "Our kaizen events have eliminated a lot of waste, but they haven't gotten to the root cause of the waste. So even though inventory is down in each department, it's as high as ever between departments."

"Aren't you being a bit hard on yourselves?" Harman said.

"I don't think so," said Dave. "It is what it is."

"Let me know if I can do anything to help," said Harman.

Chapter 9
Improving Our System

It was the beginning of December and the Atlas Industries' management team was wrapping up its yearend review. Karras had reminded the Atlas team that they were ending this year's planning and execution cycle—and beginning next year's cycle. Each deployment leader summarized the year's *Profitability*, *Delivery*, *Customer Satisfaction*, and *Employee Satisfaction* results on a one-page, current-status A3. These papers would provide the foundation for developing next year's A3 strategies.

Here is what Ed Wolf, *Profitability* deployment leader, presented:

The *Profitability* Story—Yearend

The upper part of the A3 summarized the year's *Profitability* "story" in terms of *end-of-pipe* metrics—revenue and EBIT:

A. Revenue and costs had improved:

- Atlas had exceeded its *revenue target* for the year ($255.6 million vs. $252 million) and had secured three major new coil programs worth $37 million. The NPD process had improved.

- *EBIT* had improved to 4.6 % ($11.8 million) but fell short of the target of 5% ($12.6 million). Ed explained that about $2.7 million of the gain in EBIT was related to the new business Atlas had secured and that cost reductions accounted for the rest.

- On the cost side, Atlas exceeded its cash-flow increase target ($10.1 million vs. $10 million). Atlas had partially cashed out the "hidden bank accounts" (inventory, cost of quality, operating expenses, and so on).

- Ed also pointed out that the inventory reduction that was achieved (amounting to $2.6 million) had necessitated a chargeback of about $780,000 against EBIT. "In effect, our accounting system has been hiding these costs and we've had to charge them back. That's why we're moving to *real numbers*," he said, "and away from standard cost accounting."

B. Three overall reflection points had emerged:
  - Next year Atlas has to sustain the product development process improvements, and the "market-in" philosophy.

  - Kaizen events produced varied improvement results; the kaizen process has to be improved.

  - Atlas needs an overall visual pull system.

With respect to reflection points, Ed was initially unsure about how blunt he could be. Would Deb Kramer or Dave Taylor be offended? Ed was highlighting problems in their respective zones, even though both functions had improved. Ed discussed the A3 with them in advance, and this seemed to release any latent tension. Dave was surprisingly open about the criticism of Manufacturing's kaizen events. He agreed some of them had been pretty bad.

Ed's biggest insight, gained through discussion with Karras and Dave, was the need for a visual pull system. Atlas was developing islands of stability but they weren't tied together. Work-in-process inventory proliferated between them—swelling cost and lead time.

The bottom portion of the A3 told the *Profitability* story in terms of process metrics. Goals and activities on the left column were taken directly from the right-hand side of the *Profitability* A3:

A. Better products to market quicker:

There were two yellow and three green ratings. Both NPD lead times and engineering change orders per launch had improved by 20%. NPD process improvements included the operations-NPD task force, new engineering capabilities (e.g. air quality), visual management and standards for WIP, throughput, and other process measures.

B. Reduce waste—find the hidden bank accounts:

Ed had identified five major cost reduction areas: inventory, cost of quality, operating expense, material cost, and overtime. The Atlas team had agreed to targets and means to get there (kaizen events). There were four red and one green rating. The team had found $10.4 million in savings vs. a target of $16.5 million.

With the *Next steps/Learning points* section, Ed was again initially hesitant to criticize, but relaxed after reviewing his comments in advance with his peers.

A. Better products to market quicker:

- *Prototype pilot testing was a bottleneck.* Manufacturing team members were rewarded from production—not for testing prototypes. The incentive structure had to change to create ownership for prototype testing.

- *Customer-in philosophy not well understood.* The operations-NPD task force had made better product decisions, but the group didn't really understand the customer-in philosophy. Deb had asked Ed to add this point as a challenge to NPD colleagues.

- *NPD status meetings were often long and unfocused.*

- *NPD work-in-process standards and the related visual aids had reduced cycle time and engineering overload.* As a result, NPD turnover and morale had markedly improved.

B. Reduce waste—find the hidden bank accounts:

- *Machine instability hampered inventory buffer reductions.* Atlas needed to maintain its focus on machine availability. As machine performance improved, Atlas needed an overall pull system to tie everything together.

- *Leaks and system damage continued to be the main cause of scrap.* Braze chemistry, the key to leak-proofing, was not well understood.

- *Departmental waste-reduction activities had reduced operating expenses by $2.8 million.* Atlas' challenge was to make waste reduction a "normal" activity.

- *Overtime savings compared to last year ($720,000) were less than the target.* Kaizen events required more overtime than expected.

- Atlas had realized unexpected savings of more than $1 million. Fewer temporary workers were needed for quality inspection work.

Each deployment leader would record the yearend status A3 in the electronic Book of Knowledge on the Atlas intranet.

The Atlas dashboard, which had initially been covered with red ratings at the start of the year, now included several yellow and green assessments. The color-rating system provided a visible, honest assessment, instead of the old system of hiding the "dirty little secrets": Green was on target; yellow was off target; and red was way off target. Each manager was trusted to use these colors to make the story plain to all.

The dashboard confirmed the management team's sense that *Profitability, Delivery, Customer Satisfaction* and *Employee Satisfaction* had all improved:

1. Green results:

- *Customer service* (the rate at which the right products were delivered in the right quantity at the right time) had increased by 3.4 percentage points.

- *Absenteeism* had fallen by 2.6 percentage points because the "Three Strikes" program had improved communication.

- *Turnover* among hourly and salaried staff had been reduced by 33% and 30%, respectively.

- *Revenue* had increased 3.6% due the winning of three new programs in the second half of the year.

- *Health and safety* (as measured by lost time case rate) had improved 29%.

2. Yellow results:

- *EBIT* had increased to $11.8 from $3.4 million (247% increase by dollar volume).

- *Efficiency*, as measured by cost per unit, had been improved by 13.8% and 1.7%, respectively, in tube-and-fin braze and final assembly.

- *Cost of quality* was cut by 11.5%.

- *Overtime* costs had been reduced by 12.5%; here, too, an improvement, but still short of the target.

3. Red results:

- *Inventory days* (raw material, work-in-process, and finished goods) had been decreased by 15%.

- *Build to schedule* had increased by 6.6 percentage points; an improvement but still well below the target of 90%.

- *Machine availability* had been improved by 11.8 percentage points to 68.8% (measured in aluminum-fin fabrication), but was considerably short of the 80% target.

Some Atlas management team members felt some of these assessments were harsh. "We improved EBIT to $11.8 million—a 247% improvement on last year!" said Jose Cano. "How can that be a yellow?"

"Our target was $12.6 million," said Ed.

Karras nodded. "Remember the scientific method. Our *Profitability* A3 was our hypothesis. '*We believe that these actions will achieve an EBIT of $12.6 million.*' Clearly, we need to adjust our hypothesis for next year."

What Have We Learned about Our Manufacturing Process?

Karras posed this question after the deployment leaders had reported out.

"We reduced variation in the four Ms," said Sophie. "That's why our results improved."

"Give me a breakdown," Karras said.

"Process capability improved marginally in each department," said Bob Jonas, Quality Assurance director. "But standardized work hasn't developed any roots."

"We really stabilized manpower, thanks to the good work of Phil Lucas and HR," said Dave. "Machine availability improved marginally, but it is still way below our OA target of 80%."

"Why hasn't standardized work developed roots? Why can't we stabilize our machinery?" Karras asked.

"Because we're still a firefighting culture," said Sophie.

"You can't solve problems unless you have good standards," Vic Falcone added. "But some people in my shop don't believe in standardized work or in preventive maintenance. It's just words to them."

"Under pressure," said Karras, "people do what they *know* how to do. They *know* how to fight fires. They *don't know* how to manage to standards. To change the culture, we have to change behavior. But let's leave that discussion for our next gemba session. What else have we learned?"

The team continued with their reflective conversation. Here are some more learning points they gleaned:

- ⊙ *Atlas improved because there was a compelling need for change.*
  Every year, the management team had to create a sense of urgency.

- ⊙ *Most big changes usually occur in short bursts.*
  The major system changes were done during four-day kaizen events.

⊙ *The keys to effective kaizen events are preparation and followup.*
Where kaizen events fell short of desired results, it could often be traced back to the definition of the problem being unclear. Inadequate upfront work meant that people spent a lot of time standing around. Many kaizen events generated long punch lists that were never completed. This just alienated team members who had participated and generated ideas that were never implemented.

⊙ *Getting alignment and commitment is a slow process.*
The intense kaizen activity was necessary to kick-start the change process, but it had alienated some people.

⊙ *We need to understand lean principles in our guts.*
The best way to learn was to try it on the shopfloor.

To Change Culture Change Behavior
Culture is day-to-day behavior, which follows structure. Therefore, to change its firefighting culture Atlas has to create structures that compel the right behavior.

To strengthen fundamentals like standardized work, safety, 5S, and preventive maintenance, companies like Toyota have large kamishibai (story book) audit boards on the shopfloor (see an example at right). For each operation in a zone there are slots and a card with a series of yes/no questions on it.

Group and team leaders audit an operation by observing what's actually happening and comparing it with the standard (e.g., the standardized work chart). The card for that operation is put in the slot to show that the audit has been done. When there's a problem, the card is turned over, which makes the abnormality visible at a glance (the back of the card is a different color and/or symbol). Toyota managers spend a lot of time walking the floor to verify important systems are being sustained in each area.

Kamishibai Board

All line operations

	Daily checks		Weekly/monthly checks			
	Shift 1	Shift 2	Shift 1	Shift 2	Etc.	Etc.
Operation 1						
Operation 2						
etc.						

Number of columns depends on number of items checked, checking frequency, and number of shifts

- -

CARDS

Category:	Safety and 5S	Standardized work	Quality	Preventive maintenance
Front:	Safety and 5S			
Back:	Safety			

Check details

White label to show when card is turned to highlight abnormality

For example, in a hospital laboratory, preventive maintenance (PM) on equipment such as gas chromatographs, mass spectrometers, and centrifuges is fundamental to success and often a matter of life and death. Measurement errors that result from poorly performing equipment could result in misdiagnoses. In such a medical setting, a kamishibai board could be utilized to:

- Identify the critical machines using the board, corresponding maintenance checks, and required frequency of checking.

- Write the checkpoints for each machine on a kamishibai card. (Apply visual management to the machines so that the checkpoint and purpose are obvious.)

- Determine which checks can be effectively and safely done by regular laboratory team members and which require maintenance experts.

- Train team members in the purpose, frequency, and contents of the check, and in the kamishibai process.

- Label the kamishibai board accordingly: i.e., the left column lists the critical machines and the row along the top shows the frequency (daily, weekly).

- Run a pilot and adjust the process based on what's learned. During the pilot team members practice doing maintenance checks at the required frequency. They record results and turn cards over to make abnormalities visible at a glance, helping abnormalities to get fixed quicker. Recurring abnormalities would trigger problem-solving.

Through such a process we confirm the PMs are being done, teach and confirm critical standards, and engage team members.

Next Year's Challenge—Connecting Everything with a Visual Pull System

"Here's maybe our biggest challenge for next year," Karras told them. "As Ed suggested during his report-out that we need to tie everything together with a *visual pull system*. We've made good improvements within each department. For example, our kaizen events have greatly reduced changeover time in aluminum-fin fabrication. But we're not using our new capability—changeovers aren't any more frequent. That's why we missed our inventory reduction target—there is a ton of work-in-process *between* departments.[1] If we pull this off, just watch what happens to WIP, cost, and lead time!"

"We'll have to continue to improve stability of the four Ms," Sophie insisted.

Karras nodded. "You can't pull without stability."

How Do We Improve Our Planning and Execution System?

This was Karras' next question.

"We've got to move to real numbers and plain-language accounting," Ed said. "You shouldn't need an MBA to understand our financial statements. I also had a revelation the other day—let's review our financial condition every month with all our employees. We could do it in the cafeteria. Plain-language accounting and no bull. I figure the better our employees understand our business, the better we'll be."

Karras laughed. "Ed, you're a phenomenon. That's a great idea. We'll have to confirm it with Bill, of course." Harman made a face and pretended to have a heart attack, which got a big laugh.

"Deployment leaders need a better check process," said Carrie, *Delivery* deployment leader. "I really struggled trying to keep track of our baby A3s and kaizen events."

1. For a detailed discussion of pull systems, see: Mike Rother and John Shook, *Learning to See* (Cambridge, MA, Lean Enterprise Institute, 1999), and Art Smalley, *Creating Level Pull* (Cambridge, MA, Lean Enterprise Institute, 2004).

Bob Jonas, *Customer Satisfaction* deployment leader, agreed. "We need a systematic way of tracking action plans, kaizen events, and problem-solving related to our areas of focus. My *Customer Satisfaction* dashboard was a big help, but it wasn't enough."

"We also need to link *performance appraisal* to strategy deployment," Phil said. "John, you've taught us that work has two sides to it: daily work and improvement work. A person's bonus should depend on both."

The Atlas team continued like that and came up with even more improvement ideas:

⊙ *Focus, focus, focus*: We put too much on our mother A3s this year.

⊙ *Improve the team-level check process*: Team leaders need guidance on the who, what, when, where, why, and how of checking.

⊙ *Involve team members*: Deployment often stopped at the team-leader level.

⊙ *Improve training for middle managers*: Many group leaders and team leaders felt they didn't understand the philosophy, techniques, and tools of strategy deployment.

⊙ *Strengthen problem-solving skills through on-the-job training*: Classroom learning can only go so far.

⊙ *Strengthen understanding of critical lean tools through on-the-job training*: Many group and team leaders had requested training in value-stream mapping, standardized work, and other lean tools.

⊙ *Use just-in-time training*: Implement training quickly, where it was needed.

⊙ *Develop a three-to-five-year strategy*.

Ed recorded all these ideas and would implement them in the years to come. He was the deployment leader for strategy deployment and took his role seriously.

Dave Taylor Reflects

Dave dropped into Karras' office to wish him a happy holiday. "I've learned a lot this year, John. Thanks for being patient with me."

"I'm proud of you, Dave," Karras replied. "What did you learn this year?"

"Whoa, I don't know where to start," said Dave. "Here are a few things: I don't have to *know* everything. I don't have to *control* everything. A manager's job is to practice and teach *Plan-Do-Check-Adjust*, which is hard."

Karras smiled. "My sensei used to say '*Set standards, solve problems, and treat people with respect.*' It's the same thing. Did you learn anything else?"

"Management is about *language*. Out of all the noise, we need to find the two or three critical ideas. Then we can focus and motivate people. Management is also about *leverage*. I used to run around the shopfloor thinking I had to solve everything. Because I didn't trust anybody, my team didn't grow."

"That's not a bad list," said Karras.

"There's more," said Dave. "You can be both respectful of people and intensely focused on the problem. I like your phrase 'Target. Actual. Please explain.' It takes the emotion out of checking."

Dave would have continued, but Karras, in a friendly manner, stopped him. They shook hands. Karras slapped Dave on the back and said, "Get out of here. It's the holidays."

The View from Above

At day's end, Harman invited the entire management team to his place for some "holiday cheer." Standing by the great fireplace in his fine old house, Harman raised a glass to the Atlas team. "Your yearend review meeting was the best I've attended all year. I appreciate your honesty, passion, and skill. It's been a great year, and next year will be even better. I have absolute faith in you. Thanks for everything, from the bottom of my heart."

Afterward, Harman and Karras stood at the window, looking out over snow-covered hills.

"John, there's something I need to do to improve our system," said Harman.

"What's that, Bill?"

"I need to sweeten the pot for our employees," Harman said. "I've always wanted an employee profit-sharing plan. But we've never been able to afford it."

"Bill, I like happy endings as much as the next person," Karras replied, "but maybe not just yet. We haven't much profit to share, remember."

Harman laughed. "I guess you're right, John. Must be the wine talking."

"No, it's not the wine," said Karras. "You're just a good man."

The View from the Floor

Karras and Tom Schmidt were having a souvlaki lunch at the Imperial Bar & Grill.

"This is quite a place, John," said Tom, eyeing the unconventional Christmas decorations.

"I grew up in a Greek restaurant," Karras told him. "So tell me, how did we do this year?"

"Overall, I think we did pretty well," Tom replied. "Some people thought we had too many kaizen events, and others didn't like it when their ideas were ignored. But on the whole, team members feel that we're moving in a good direction. I think most people are pretty happy that management is trying to make their jobs easier."

"Anything we can do to get better next year?" Karras asked.

"Just keep doing what you're doing. I see a real difference in Dave Taylor. I think he really respects you, and us."

"Dave has worked hard," said Karras, "and so have you. Have some feta cheese."

Epilogue

And so ended Atlas Industries first annual strategy deployment cycle. In the years to come the Atlas team got increasingly better at planning and execution—and at lean thinking. Strategy deployment helped Atlas focus on and quickly deliver lean tools to its biggest problems. Soon standardized work, pull, flow, visual management, etc., were no big deal. They were just how Atlas did business.

Atlas began to develop interesting new products:

⊙ Coils and condensers designed for the computer, healthcare, and pharmaceutical industries,

⊙ Coils and condensers coated with proprietary materials that prevented mold growth, and

⊙ Air cleaning technologies, like ultraviolet and electrostatic treatment systems.

Atlas also was able to make these products in smaller batches and with shorter lead times than the competition. Atlas did more business at good margins with wholesalers. Even the OEMs took notice, which is why Jack Henderson wanted to play golf with Harman. He wanted to work with Atlas again. And that's where this story began.

The Big Questions

How does your organization review and reflect on yearend results?

How does your organization record and build on yearend results?

How does your organization check and confirm critical management processes?

Who owns the planning and execution system at your organization?

What does your organization do to improve its planning and execution system each year?

Appendix A
A Better Approach to Planning and Execution

For nowhere in the planning literature has there been any indication whatsoever that efforts were made to understand how the strategy-making process really does work in organizations.

—Henry Mintzberg[1]

Why is the way we plan and execute so screwed up— and how do we fix it?

At the dawn of the 20th century, an American named Frederick Taylor applied the scientific method to the chaotic world of work. By formally studying routine jobs—shoveling coal, for example—Taylor vastly improved the efficiency and quality of manual work. He proposed that, by careful observation, the "one best way" could be found for such work. Taylor thereby invented industrial engineering and laid the foundation for the mass-production system.

Half a century later, post-World War II academic theorists had a brain-wave: *"If Taylor's methods work on the factory floor, maybe they can work in the executive suite, too."* The academics were especially interested in planning and execution. If we can find the "one best way" to plan and execute, they reasoned, senior management can coordinate the big picture; much like a chess player coordinates the pieces on a chessboard.

1. Henry Mintzberg, *The Rise and Fall of Strategic Planning*, (New York, The Free Press, 1994).

A bold idea, to be sure, and the academics ran with it. They produced a series of planning models whose complexity was overwhelming.[2]

The Fallacy of Formalization

But the academics missed Taylor's fundamental message: before you can standardize a process, you have to *understand* it. To develop standardized work for a factory process, for example, you have to "go see" and grasp its elements and their sequence, duration, and spatial arrangement. By contrast, the "Planning School" models tell you everything—except how to develop a strategy.

The Fallacy of Detachment

Detachment is a core Planning School assumption; the idea that we benefit by "abstracting" management from day-to-day operations. But strategic plans developed at "central command" are often divorced from reality. During the Vietnam war, for example, Secretary of Defense Robert MacNamara and his staff developed military strategies from Washington, remote from the battlefields and absent any knowledge of the true nature of warfare.[3]

Detachment creates an overreliance on "hard" data, which often means that financial data crowds out everything else. But the endless corporate-accounting scandals suggest the hard numbers aren't so hard after all.

2. Henry Mintzberg, *The Rise and Fall of Strategic Planning*, (New York, The Free Press, 1994).
3. Col. Harry G. Summers Jr., *On Strategy: A Critical Analysis of the Vietnam War* (Novato, CA, Presidio Press, 1982).

The Grand Fallacy

Conventional planning is all analysis (left brain). But the essence of strategy is *not* analysis—it's the *synthesis* of analysis and *intuition*. Intuition helps us answer questions like:

- What is the mood in the plant?

- What did the look on the supplier's face mean?

- How are we viewed in the market relative to our competitors?

Thus, strategy engages both the left and the right (creative) brain. The result is a compelling narrative, a story. We need to be able to tell *persuasive stories*—to our managers and team members, to our customers and suppliers, to our development partners, and to the investment community.

The Planning School reached its zenith between 1960 and 1990. One wonders how much corporate life it has killed. The Japanese strategist Ohmae has this to say:

"Most large U.S. corporations are run like the Soviet Union economy ... with their emphasis on central plans and the details which spell out expectations for managers' actions, ... a remarkably effective way of killing creativity and entrepreneurship."[4]

The command-and-control school, at root, seeks to turn people into predictable automata. It's a loser's game. Even totalitarian states fail in the end, despite overwhelming propaganda and coercion. Human beings are simply too complex, idiosyncratic, and cranky. Command and control debases our team members. They lose part of their humanity. We lose their knowledge, experience, and creativity. Half a century ago, Taiichi Ohno, founder of the Toyota Production System, saw the same sad waste on the Toyota shopfloor. "What a terrible waste of humanity," he said.

4. Kiichiro Ohmae, *The Mind of the Strategist*, (New York, McGraw-Hill, 1982).

The Planning School has been discredited, but its legacy lingers in the dysfunctional mental models of our supervisors, managers, and executives. Look no further than the wildly successful *Dilbert* comic.

Drucker and Juran

Peter Drucker and Joseph Juran were beacons of clarity during the Planning School's heyday. Strategy deployment is built on the foundation laid by Drucker's *The Practice of Management*[5] and Juran's *Managerial Breakthrough*.[6] Drucker posed critical questions in an accessible way:[7]

- What should a company's overall objectives be?

- What should a manager's objectives be?

- How do we create objectives?

- How do we control (check) results against our objectives?

- How do we manage by objectives, instead of by exhortation?

Drucker's answers created the practical planning system called Management by Objectives (MBO), whose innovations were many:

- Objectives form a hierarchy (tree).

- We must align objectives level by level.

- A company's objectives must be balanced; profit alone is an inadequate metric.

- There should be an annual planning cycle during which actual results and objectives can be compared.

5. Peter Drucker, *The Practice of Management*, (New York, McGraw-Hill, 1954).
6. Joseph Juran, *Managerial Breakthrough*, (New York, McGraw-Hill, 1964).
7. Peter Drucker, *The Practice of Management*, (New York, McGraw-Hill, 1954).

Juran called his system Strategic Quality Planning and it entailed the deployment of objectives and policies. Juran's innovations included:

⊙ Setting broad quality goals by senior management,

⊙ Deploying quality goals and policies level by level,

⊙ Cross-functionality through "quality committees" (to erode silos),

⊙ Annual planning cycle based on the PDCA cycle,

⊙ Assessment of end-of-pipe and process measures,

⊙ Problem-solving using the scientific method, and

⊙ Involvement through shopfloor quality circles.

Juran continued to refine his system and extended it to design for quality.[8] Few North American companies paid attention.

Drucker and Juran greatly influenced Japanese corporations who hungrily absorbed and refined their ideas. The term "hoshin kanri" was first used by Bridgestone Tire in 1964. Around the same time, Masao Nemoto began to develop Toyota's annual planning and execution system.[9]

How Is Strategy Deployment Different?

Strategy deployment seeks to answer the critical strategic planning questions in simple, compelling ways:

⊙ Who are we?

⊙ Where are we going?

⊙ How do we get there?

8. Joseph Juran, *Juran on Quality by Design*, (New York, The Free Press, 1992).
9. Masao Nemoto, *Total Quality Control for Management—Strategies and Techniques from Toyota and Toyoda Gosei*,(Englewood Cliffs, NJ, Prentice Hall, 1987).

The journey is a useful metaphor. Our current-state value-stream map is "where we are," and our future-state map is "where we want to go." The "kaizen bursts" on our current-state map are analogous to "boulders" (e.g., major flow or capability problems that we need to fix). The "small stones" are the day-to-day management issues that we need to solve.

Strategy deployment provides a broad umbrella structure that allows the Plan-Do-Check-Adjust cycle—the scientific method—to flourish. It seeks to balance the benefits of centralized control with the need for autonomy and initiative. Strategy deployment provides for "bottom-up" involvement, tapping into a vast knowledge reservoir and diluting the *Dilbert* effect. Why shouldn't work be fun?

How does strategy deployment fit into the lean production system? Think of it as the brain and nervous system.

Brain:

⊙ Tells interesting stories.

⊙ Applies scientific method (PDCA).

⊙ Reflects and learns.

Nervous System:

⊙ Aligns activity.

⊙ Connects everything.

⊙ Responds quickly.

Through strategy deployment we seek to achieve:

- ⊙ *Focus*—What are our critical few goals?
- ⊙ *Alignment*—How do we get all the players on the same page (literally)?
- ⊙ *Quick response*—How do we make problems visible to everyone so that we can respond quickly?

We don't want robots, moving in lock step. We want human beings, in all their creative cranky and eccentric glory, moving in the same direction, pulled by a shared vision.

Focus, Alignment, and Quick Response

Before strategy deployment
(management by milling around)

After strategy deployment

Appendix B
Atlas Industries A3 Strategies

The respective deployment leaders—Carrie Webb, Bob Jonas, and Phil Lucas—followed a process similar to the one Ed Wolf followed in developing his *Profitability* A3: They reviewed the relevant value-stream maps, went to the gemba, and talked with their colleagues. In keeping with their "chief scientist" role, they made and sought support for their diagnoses and led action planning. Their role wasn't easy; they had to ask tough questions and challenge existing assumptions. There were difficult moments; some department managers resented being challenged. All the A3s required several revisions before everyone was on the same page.

An important part of strategy deployment is growing strong deployment leaders, who help us develop the creative tension necessary to acknowledge and address deeply rooted problems. The first year or so is the most challenging. Perhaps the most common failure is collapsing the tension by sweeping problems under the carpet. Deployment leaders often become unpopular the first year and get "barbequed" on occasion.

At the outset of Atlas Industries' strategy deployment, in Chapter 5, the initial *Profitability* A3 strategy is described. *Delivery, Customer Satisfaction,* and *Employee Satisfaction* A3 strategies and the stories are included here:

A3 Intuitive Flow

Strategy A3 Theme

- What strategic objectives do we need to achieve this year?
- How did we do last year?
- What's our history?

- What did we do last year?
- What worked and didn't work?
- What have we learned?

- What do we need to do to achieve this year's strategic objectives?
- How will these actions benefit us?

- What's our action plan to achieve these objectives (who, what, when, where, and how)?

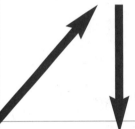

- Are there any unresolved issues?
- Do you need any help with anything?
- Anything bothering you?

Focus: Delivery

Excellence in Delivery

Performance, gaps, and targets

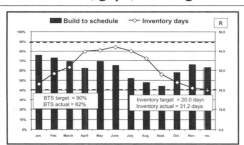

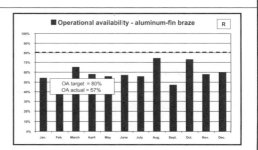

Last year: BTS target = 90.0%
BTS actual = 62.0%

This year: Inventory target = 20.C days
($6.3 million)

Last year: Availability target = 80.0%
Availability actual = 57.0%

This year: Availability target = 80.0%

Reflection on last year's activities

Activity	Rating	Key results / issues
Implemented BTS metric	G	Problems now visible: downtime and scrap
Implemented availability tracking	G	Hot spots: aluminum-fin fab A and C stackers Tube and fin fab: klamming benders
Maintenance cross-training	R	Target: full coverage bcth shifts; little progress "No time for training"
Maintenance problem-solving	R	Training too complex; 'not usable"

Analysis / Justification to this year's activities

Last year we made our Delivery problems visible, but couldn't solve them.

Firefighting hampers maintenance cross-training and system building.

Biggest losses: changeover and breakdowns. Next year need to:

1) Strengthen maintenance planning process (e.g. work-order scheduling board).

2) Buffer stacking and bending machine losses with manual backup.

3) Reduce changeover times.

4) Improve maintenance versatility and reduce attrition.

Signatures:

Thi

Goa

A. S
p

Wor

B. R
attr

Red

C. R
c

Red
Red

D. R
p

Red
to 2

Fo

1. H

2. I

3.

Dept: PC & L

s year's action plan

ls	Activities	J	F	M	A	M	J	J	A	S	O	N	D
trengthen maintenance anning process	1. Design and pilot work-order board	█											
	2. Confirm process and launch		█	█									
	3. Track % of projects complete (PPC)				█	█	█	█	█	█	█	█	█
Targets	4. Weekly maintenance plan based on				█	█	█	█	█	█	█	█	█
k-order board March 30	PPC reflection												
educe maintenance ition; improve versatility	1. Pilot "Grow with Us" incentive program	█											
	2. Set up versatility boards; schedule shops				█								
Targets	3. Implement "Mentor" program						█						
ce attrition to < 5%													
educe downtime and hangeover time	1. Develop manual backup for three machines in each department	█											
	2. Train team member in backup procedures				█	█	█						
Targets	3. Focused kaizen events — changeover reduction									█	█	█	
ce C/O 25%													
ce D/T 25%													
educe in-plant inventory roblem-solving process	1. Link material management system to consumption	█	█	█	█	█	█						
	2. Apply visual management to lineside inventory (focus: final assembly)				█	█	█						
Targets	3. Pilot pull systems in final assembly (five high-volume parts)						█	█	█				
ce on-hand inventory 0 days	4. Confirm and stabilize pull loops							█	█	█	█	█	
		J	F	M	A	M	J	J	A	S	O	N	D

lowup / Unresolved issues

How to diffuse tension between manufacturing and maintenance?

Manual backup and quick changeover requires good grasp of standardized work.
— Enhance training

Making work order status visible is a major cultural shift for maintenance. How to prepare?

Author: Carrie Webb
Version and date: V7

Delivery

Carrie's *Delivery* A3 focused on machine instability, and its underlying causes: a weak maintenance-planning process, poor maintenance versatility and teamwork, and sloppy changeover practices. By stabilizing machinery, Carrie hoped to help reduce the in-plant inventory buffer by *$4.5 million*, in accord with Ed Wolf's *Profitability* strategy.

Carrie recognized that inventory also grew unchecked because the material management system was not linked to consumption or to the fledgling pull systems. She also learned about the tension between Manufacturing and maintenance, the high maintenance-attrition rates, and the absence of visual management on work orders.

Initially Carrie's strategy also targeted outgoing logistics. She wanted to apply the lean logistics concepts she had recently learned. Upon reflection and discussion, she decided to defer this activity until in-plant delivery had stabilized.

Carrie had many chats with Dave Taylor, Manufacturing director, and his team about all of these issues. After much give-and-take they agreed on targets for process metrics like inventory turns, machine downtime, and changeover time. She also spoke with Phil Lucas, *Employee Satisfaction* deployment leader, about an idea for a program she called "Grow With Us," which Carrie believed could help reduce maintenance attrition rates.

Focus: Employee Satisfaction   **Strengthening HR Proce**

Performance, gaps, and targets

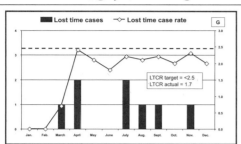

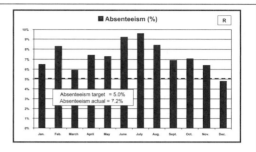

Last year: LTCR target = 2.0
     LTCR actual = 1.7

This year: LTCR target = 2.0

Last year: Absenteeism target = 5.0%
      Absenteeism actual = 7.2%

This year: Absenteeism target = 5.0%

Goa

A. R
  P

All C
by S

B. S
  t

20 a

C. R
  t
  (

One
Com
all d

D. T
  p

Reflection on last year's activities

Activity	Rating	Key results / issues
Implemented observation-based safety (OBS)	G	Fewer incidents; more involvement
Implemented "Three Strikes" program	R	Did we communicate well?
Turnover-reduction plan	R	Targets: hourly = 5%; salary = 5% Actuals: hourly = 6.8%; salary =11.2%
Problem-solving training	R	Target: All group leaders certified Actual: four of 17 certified Training was "waste of time"

Analysis / Justification to this year's activities

We're losing key people. Exit interviews cite overtime, anxiety over future, and heat in summer.

Absenteeism causes of production loss. Three Strikes policy badly planned. (GL involvement?)

Observation-based safety involved employees. How to leverage? This year we need to:

  1) Relaunch Three Strikes policy. Involve group leaders up front.

  2) Use OBS as conduit for broader team member involvement and problem-solving.

  3) Reduce overtime through kaizen and communicate clear direction to reduce turnover.

  4) Teach and apply a simpler problem-solving process.

Signatures:

year's action plan

s	Activities	J	F	M	A	M	J	J	A	S	O	N	D
aunch Three Strikes ogram	1. Feedback sessions with GLs and TLs	■											
	2. Adjust training and implementation plan		■										
	3. Pilot new training; adjust per feedback			■									
Targets	4. Full implementation				■	■	■	■	■	■	■	■	■
s and TLs certified pt. 30													
rengthen Involvement rough OBS	1. Expand training to all departments	■											
	2. Set up OBS boards in each shop		■										
	3. Teach problem-solving to core				■	■							
Targets	OBS members												
dits/GL/month	4. Extend problem-solving training							■	■				
duce turnover 25% rough communication ocus: business plan)	1. Communication boards in all departments	■											
	2. Post A3 strategies and monthly		■	■	■	■	■	■	■	■	■	■	■
	dashboard												
	3. Strengthen Town Hall meeting		■	■	■	■	■	■	■	■	■	■	■
Targets	4. Ensure kaizen events target overtime	■											
own Hall per month	reduction												
munication boards in partments													
ach and apply simple oblem-solving process	1. Identify different problem-solving	■											
	approaches												
	2. Pilot training and adjust per feedback			■									
	3. Train all TLs and above					■							
	4. Develop support processes							■	■	■	■	■	■
	(database, etc.)												
		J	F	M	A	M	J	J	A	S	O	N	D

lowup / Unresolved issues

eed to improve Hot Work plan for hot summer months.

eed to generate sense of optimism about plant's future.

hree Strikes program may result in termination of repeat offenders.
– Monitor for morale effect.

Author: **Phil Lucas**
Version and date: V4

Appendix C
Templates

The following templates are also available as full-size downloads from the Lean Enterprise Institute. Go to *lean.org/grtd*.

Getting the Right Things Done

Lean Enterprise Institute

Continue Your Learning

The Lean Enterprise Institute (LEI) has a wide range of learning resources, all with the practical knowledge you need to sustain a lean transformation:

Learning Materials

Our plain-language books, workbooks, leadership guides, and training materials reflect the essence of lean thinking—doing. They draw on years of research and real-world experiences from lean transformations in manufacturing and service organizations to provide tools that you can put to work immediately.

Education

Faculty members with extensive implementation experience teach you actual applications with the case studies, work sheets, formulas, and methodologies you need for implementation. Select from courses that address technical topics, culture change, coaching, senior management's roles, and much more.

Events

Every March the Lean Transformation Summit explores the latest lean concepts and case studies, presented by executives and implementers. Other events focus on an issue or industry, such as starting a lean transformation or implementing lean in healthcare. Check lean.org for details and to get first notice of these limited-attendance events.

Feedback

We've tried to make this guide easy to understand with detailed instructions, simple illustrations, and clear examples. However, we know from years of experience that applying even the simplest concept in a complex organization is difficult. So we need your help. After you have tried implementing the techniques described in strategy deployment, please mail, fax, or email your comments to:

Lean Enterprise Institute
One Cambridge Center
Cambridge, MA 02142 USA

Fax: (617) 871-2999
Email: grtd@lean.org
Web: lean.org

Ohmae, Kiichiro, *The Mind of the Strategist*, New York: McGraw-Hill, 1982.

Rother, Mike and John Shook, *Learning to See*, Cambridge, MA: Lean Enterprise Institute, 1999.

Rother, Mike and Rick Harris, *Creating Continuous Flow*, Cambridge, MA: Lean Enterprise Institute, 2001.

Smalley, Art , *Creating Level Pull*, Cambridge, MA: Lean Enterprise Institute, 2004.

Spear, Steven and Kent Bowen, "Decoding the DNA of the Toyota Production System," *Harvard Business Review*, October/November 1999.

Summers Jr., Col. Harry G., *On Strategy: A Critical Analysis of the Vietnam War*, Novato, CA: Presidio Press, 1982.

Bibliography

Brassard, Michael and Diane Ritter, *The Memory Jogger II*, *A Pocket Guide of Tools for Continuous Improvement and Effective Planning*, Methuen, MA, Goal/QPC, 1994.

Dennis, Pascal, *Andy and Me—Crisis and Transformation on the Lean Journey*, University Park, IL: Productivity Press, 2005.

Drucker, Peter, *The Practice of Management*, New York: McGraw-Hill, 1954.

Fiume, Orest, Jean E. Cunningham, with Emily Adams, *Real Numbers: Management Accounting in a Lean Organization*: Managing Times Press, Durham, NC, 2003.

Juran, Joseph, *Managerial Breakthrough*, New York: McGraw-Hill, 1964.

Juran, Joseph, *Juran on Quality by Design*, New York: The Free Press, 1992.

Marchwinski, Chet, and John Shook, editors, *Lean Lexicon*, Cambridge, MA: Lean Enterprise Institute, January 2003.

Maskell, Brian and Bruce Baggaley, *Practical Lean Accounting: A Proven System for Measuring and Managing in a Lean Enterprise*, University Park, IL: Productivity Press, 2003.

Mintzberg, Henry, *The Rise and Fall of Strategic Planning*, New York: The Free Press, 1994.

Nemoto, Masao, *Total Quality Control for Management—Strategies and Techniques from Toyota and Toyoda Gosei*, Englewood Cliffs, NJ: Prentice Hall, 1987.

About the Author

Pascal Dennis is a professional engineer, author, and adviser to North American firms making the lean leap. Pascal developed his skills on the Toyota shopfloor in North America and Japan and by working with major international companies. He is a faculty member of the Lean Enterprise Institute.

Pascal has been a manager of operations; human resources; finance; and health, safety, and environment. He has supported lean implementation at leading international companies in sectors as diverse as automotive, the process industries, heavy equipment, construction, and healthcare. The focus of his lean practice is strategic planning and execution (strategy deployment); quality, delivery, and cost management; health and safety; and business process improvement.

In leadership positions at Toyota Motor Manufacturing Canada (TMMC), Pascal supported several major model launches, the construction of a new 3-million square-foot facility, and the hiring of 2,000 new team members.

Pascal has received the ASQ Golden Quill, OSH Award of Excellence, and other awards. Pascal's previous book, the business novel *Andy and Me— Crisis and Transformation on the Lean Journey*,[10] won a 2006 Shingo Prize.

10. Pascal Dennis, *Andy and Me—Crisis and Transformation on the Lean Journey*, (University Park, IL, Productivity Press, 2005).

le Party	Target Date	J	F	M	A	M	J	J	A	S	O	N	D	Review	Review

Dept:

		J	F	M	A	M	J	J	A	S	O	N	D		

Actual start	◇ Review	◯	On target
Proposed start	△ Proposed completion	△	Behind target
Actual completion	✖		Trouble

Focus:	Action Plan	Objective:		
Task No.	Task		Metric	Responsib

Prepared by:

Revision number and date:

Signatures:

Current-Status A3 / Yearend Review

Focus/Goal: _____   **Deployment leader** _____

	Overview	Target	Actual	Rating	Comments
Goal					
Targets					
Activities					

		YTD Results		Rating	Comments / Concerns	Next steps / Learning points
		Target	Actual			

Current-Status A3 / Yearend Review Template

A current-status or yearend review A3 is a one-page storyboard on 11-inch by 17-inch paper that summarizes the status of an important strategic planning initiative, such as our *Customer Satisfaction* strategy. Normally, we use them at our midyear and yearend strategic planning reviews.

The yearend review A3 comprises two main boxes: the top box provides an overview of how we're doing with respect to our critical end-of-pipe metrics (e.g. revenue, profit, customer delivery, quality rates, lost time injury rate, etc.) including the target and actual measures, a rating, and a brief explanation. The second box provides an overview of our activities, and usually reflects what's been prescribed on the action plan of the right side of our strategy A3. Again, we provide activity targets and actual measures, ratings, explanations, and next steps. Here are some dos and don'ts:

Do:

- ⊙ Highlight how you're doing with respect to the critical needs and gaps you are trying to address.

- ⊙ Reflect honestly on what's happened so far this year (or this half-year). What worked? What didn't work? Why or why not? What have we learned? What do we do now?

- ⊙ Summarize comments, concerns, and next steps in short bullet points.

- ⊙ Discuss anything that's bothering you, such as, unresolved issues, needed resources, possible risks, and what you might do about these conditions.

- ⊙ Make it readable. Minimize the verbiage. Hold the A3 at arm's length. Does it look like something you'd like to read?

- ⊙ Rehearse your presentation.

Don't:

- ⊙ Try to hide bad news; we learn more from failure than from success.

- ⊙ Try to cram too much on your strategy A3. Strategy is about emphasis. What will you focus on?

- ⊙ Get too fancy with graphics. Remember the point of A3 thinking is to develop a shared understanding so we can solve problems and get results.

- ⊙ Use tiny fonts that make the A3 impossible to read.

- ⊙ Use jargon. Please use plain language.

- ⊙ Bore people during your presentations. You have 10 minutes at most to tell your story, so rehearse to make the best impression.